T0146626

G.I. Resister

the story of how one American
Soldier and his family fought
the
War in Vietnam

Dick Perrin
With
Tim McCarthy

Order this book online at www.trafford.com
or email orders@trafford.com

Most Trafford titles are also available at major online book retailers.

Print information available on the last page.

ISBN: 978-1-5521-2851-0 (sc)

Trafford rev. 01/23/2020

 www.trafford.com

North America & international
toll-free: 1 888 232 4444 (USA & Canada)
fax: 812 355 4082

Thanks to the people who helped me to write this book:

My mother, Betty Perrin
My brother, David Perrin
My sister, Nancy Perrin
My brother, Ron Perrin
My sister-in-law, Sandra Perrin
My daughter, Ashley Perrin
Kate Penner
Bill Livant
Russ Shaw
Sheila Brass
Louise Ransom
Darlene Schiller-Oudot
Joan Skinner
Joe Jones

Special thanks
To
Tim McCarthy

These people encouraged me to keep working on this project, thank you:

Shayne Perrin
Ashley Perrin
Gregory Perrin
Walter LaVallee
Ray Kennedy
Karen Howe
Gloria Pohjavouri
Marlin Pohjavouri
Judy Saint
Doug Blatter
Joan Bauer
Hilary Harper
Bob Howard
Ellen Keewatin
John Roberts
Greg Chatterson
Cheryl Wajunta
Terry Klug
LaVerne Vollman
Tim Closson
Pat Closson
Mark Wartman
Paul Locke
Jeanne Locke
John Waite
Michael Laliberte

These people have a special interest in Vietnam War history and took time to look at my project and offer encouragement, thanks:

Prof. John Israel, University of Virginia
Ron Frankum, Ph. D. Vietnam Archives, Texas Tech
Betty Dessants, Ph.D.   Florida State University
George Herring, Ph.D. University of Kentucky
Paul Atwood, Ph.D.   Joiner Center, Univ. of Mass., Boston
Prof. Harvard Sitkoff, University of New Hampshire
Barbara Garson, author

For my children

Shayne   Ashley   Gregory

Dedicated to my Mom and Dad

Contents

FOREWORD

By Tim McCarthy

There are some books that have to be written and this is one of them. That is what finally convinced me to help Dick Perrin put the book together. I had my doubts at first—not about the book, but about the time I would have to give to it. I have a day job editing a newspaper in New Hampshire and three books of my own that I am trying to work on. But Dick's story is compelling, for many reasons. One is that it is a damn good tale, a *bildungsroman* straight from life and from the heart.

Another and ultimately larger reason has to do with a nation so deeply cleaved by the ill-fated and unjust war in Vietnam that a generation after the Paris peace process brought it formally to an end, the country has only just begun to heal. Dick's story is a part of that, a microcosm of it in many ways, both in the hurt and the healing. His mother was a nurse, his father a barber in a small Vermont town. The family could hardly have been more middle American. What the Vietnam War did to it, it did to us all.

Then there is my personal involvement in this story, a small role, to be sure, but important to me nonetheless. Dick is my

1

cousin. His father was my mother's brother. Dick and I were together with his half brother Ron in California after Dick graduated from high school in 1966, only months before he joined the army. Bored with graduate school, I had left with the intention of writing full time. Jeannine, the French woman I was married to at the time, helped me to do that. Dick was still in California when Jeannine and I left for Europe in January 1967.

Jeannine landed a civil service job at the U.S. European command headquarters in Heidelberg, Germany. Soon I found myself living in splendid isolation on a hill overlooking the village of Heiligkreuzsteinach, about a half hour north of Heidelberg. Shunning the advice of one of my major mentors, Albert Camus, I was not an artist "engaged" in the political arena. I had made a deliberate decision to divorce myself from the antiwar movement and concentrate on my work, which at that time was a huge novel that would take me six years to write. What I heard about the war came from the radio and the Paris edition of the *Herald Tribune*.

And there was also the correspondence with my friend and cousin Ron. He kept me informed about what was happening to Dick, including his antiwar activities and the court-martial at Fort Sill, the stockade time, and Dick's transfer to Germany. As you will later read, Ron's influence on Dick was deep and decisive.

Then came that sunny Sunday morning in September 1967. Jeannine's sister was visiting us in Germany and we were getting ready to take her back to France. The phone rang and Dick was on the line. That was no great surprise. I had been expecting to hear from him once he settled into his new assignment. He said he was at a hotel nearby and could I come and pick him up. Thinking that he must have had a pass for the Labor Day weekend, I hopped into the baby blue Fiat and headed straight across the valley to the hotel. It was a grand reunion.

On the way home, Dick told me that he was not going back. Not going back? "No, I'm not going back." I was silent for a time and he seemed to take that as a sign of disapproval. "You don't have to get involved if you don't want to," he said. But I told him I was only thinking about how we might manage it and that, as it happened, we were heading for France that afternoon. Still, there was a cold sensation gripping my gut that reminded me that deserting the military, especially in wartime, was serious business and that young Dick Perrin was taking a possibly irrevocable leap that would land him God knows where.

I'll leave it to Dick to tell how we got across the French border that afternoon, but there is a touch he says he has forgotten. In my mother-in-law's apartment in Verdun, three rooms in a stone building hundreds of years old, running water but the only toilet in the rear courtyard three floors down, a coal stove in every room for heat. Dick and I stepped out onto the little balcony overlooking the rue du Ru. Plastered on a wall across the street was an election poster for the Communist Party. Dick spread his arms and said, "What a country!" What a country indeed. He would get to know several sides of it in the months to come. The next day we left for Paris.

Back in Germany, I kept in touch with Dick over the weeks that followed. Then came a phone call from Max, one of the people who helped Dick and a lot of other American deserters in France. He said he wanted to meet me and he would be at the Heidelberg railroad station the next evening. "I'll be with a tall, redheaded woman and carrying a folded newspaper," he said. Max was like that. He seemed to enjoy the cloak-and-dagger stuff immensely and his love for it turned out to be infectious.

I went to the station as scheduled and there they were, an unmistakable pair, the woman, Max's friend June, about two heads taller than he was as I recall, pudgy Max in his trench coat (what else?), the newspaper folded under his arm as he chomped on a wurst. They followed me back to our place in their car and we drank beer and talked politics deep into the night. Max was probing me, checking me out, trying to sense if I could be trusted, and he was good at it.

Later I showed them a shortcut to the autobahn that would take them west. I stopped near the on-ramp and Max pulled up beside me. June reached out of the window and I grasped her hand. "I hope we see you again soon," she said. "Me too," I said. But it never happened.

What did happen was a flux of antiwar material arriving in my mailbox every week, some of it published by RITA, the war resistance group Dick helped to found. Apparently I had passed muster with Max. I began distributing the literature wherever I could. My ID card gave me access to the Heidelberg headquarters and I left the pamphlets there, in restrooms, under windshield wipers, even in the Army dentist's office when I had a cavity filled. Max called and said he wanted me to meet with students in Frankfurt. He said I would have to use a nom de guerre. With biblical pomp that I later found comical, I chose the name "Joseph."

I went to Frankfurt one gloomy Saturday afternoon, met with German students in a ratty apartment with dirty mattresses every which way on the floor, books and papers piled all about. Nobody trusted anyone else, but I ended up helping them all the same by drafting some antiwar pamphlets directed at American troops. That, too, was serious business, I know, but it was also great fun.

My routine was to start writing before dawn and sometimes nap after a walk in the afternoon. One afternoon I woke from a nap and found a man in a dark blue suit rifling the papers in my study. He had come in off the rear patio and apparently thought no one was home. Surprised, he identified himself as an Army intelligence officer. I told him to get the hell out and he did.

Soon after I learned from the son of the village postmaster that my telephone was tapped and my mail being read. He was home on break from his university in Berlin, where he was involved in the student antiwar movement. He said that each day an American agent came out from Heidelberg, took my mail with him and returned the next day. He said Americans still had the right to do that under post-World War II agreements.

So there I was, despite myself and thanks in large part to Dick Perrin, an "engaged" artist after all. And, to one degree or another, I have been ever since.

Not long after the turbulent events in France in May and June 1968, Dick left for Canada and I did not hear from him directly for almost thirty years. Then in early 1996 he called me out of the blue, said he wanted to write his story and asked me to help him with it.

In June 1996, Dick and I spent a few days together at his family's camp on a lake in southwestern Vermont. We went over his manuscript page by page while I coaxed him for details and helped him flesh out the holes in his memory. At night we cooked, drank wine, smoked the cigars he had brought from Canada, almost always with the tape recorder running. I came away with many hours of tape and a renewed friendship with Dick.

That weekend we went to Dick's high school class reunion. Dick was apprehensive, having little idea how his old classmates would receive him, a deserter still living in exile.

The reunion was across the Connecticut River in Charleston, New Hampshire, at a 200-year-old building called the Shutter Inn. This was early American indeed and somehow the site seemed appropriate.

We arrived early and when the bar opened we went in and had a beer. As luck would have it, the first member of the class of '66 to join us at the bar was a career Navy man, recently retired, a loud, chesty fellow wearing a gold necklace, so full of himself that it seemed his short frame could barely contain it. His new wife was at least twenty years his junior, a tall blonde woman who smiled almost constantly and said almost nothing. Dick and I looked at each other and smiled as if to say, "Well, here we go."

Later Russ Shaw showed up. He had been one of Dick's closest friends in high school. We went out onto the terrace and I interviewed him.

Shortly after the interview with Russ, I left and headed home. As I drove north along the river, I could not escape the feeling that, whatever happened at the reunion that night, in some distinctive way Dick Perrin had come home at last, or at least full circle from those Vietnam days. That was a happy thought, a flight of wishful thinking, perhaps, but it is clear to me now that it is going to take more than a generation for most of us to close that circle.

EVENTS OF MAY   1968

When what some called the second French Revolution was building steam that spring of 1968, I had been living in Paris for going on a year, after leaving my Army unit in Germany as a protest against the war in Vietnam. As it turned out it wasn't really a revolution, but there were moments when we thought it might have been and it did bring about some changes.

I was nineteen years old and the world was in a whirl that year. Sometimes I still find it hard to believe that I was so caught up in it. Led in large part by students, the political unrest was global. In Vietnam, there was the Tet offensive and the war was at its savage worst. Martin Luther King was assassinated that spring and later Robert Kennedy. American cities burned.

Early in May, I was asked to attend a meeting at the Sorbonne and say a few words. I was told some students from Nanterre would be there to talk about some problems on their campus. Often I was asked to speak at meetings and rallies of leftist groups to represent the American exile community of the Vietnam War era.

When I arrived at the university, there was a throng of students in the courtyard. Apparently, they had been locked out and they were not a happy lot. I was introduced to the leader, one of the students from Nanterre. His name was Daniel Cohn-Bendit and over the next few weeks his reputation would become international. He said there had been a change in plans as the school officials were not being cooperative. I would not be speaking after all.

Before I could leave, a group of right-wing students gathered outside. It wasn't safe to pass through a bunch like that. They called themselves Occident and were well known for their violent behavior. I thought I'd better wait for things to cool down.

Trouble is, it took several weeks for things to cool down. The students in the courtyard felt threatened by the group outside and began talking about defending themselves. Then they broke into the building and hauled out some chairs and desks. The chairs were smashed for makeshift clubs and the desks stacked to barricade the courtyard doors, the doors that led out to the street.

Cohn-Bendit climbed onto a desk and launched into a rousing speech that fired up the students for battle. Word spread that the police had arrived, but I was told not to worry because the police in France never entered learning institutions. Except during the Nazi occupation, the students said, the French police respected intellectual freedom and had not entered a university since the Revolution of 1789.

Never say never, as the old saying goes. The police rammed the doors open and stormed into the courtyard. Realizing they were outnumbered and ill-equipped, the students dropped their clubs and surrendered. For some reason the police separated the men from the women.

We were lined up and filed toward one of the doors opening onto the street. IDs were checked at the door. Some students were arrested, but most were released. When I was almost to the door, a student who realized my special predicament spotted me and slapped his forehead in exasperation.

He called to a professor standing nearby and the professor came over. (I learned later that he was the philosopher Paul Ricoeur and that he was a major academic figure in Europe at the time.) The student whispered in his ear. Then the professor approached one of the policemen in charge and told him I was his teaching assistant and not part of the student protest. I was allowed to leave with the professor.

We went into the building and he told me to wait for him there in the long corridor and he would be right back. I waited for what seemed like forever. Suddenly, the police appeared at the other end of the corridor. No more waiting for the professor. I opened the nearest door and went in to what turned out to be a lecture theater where a meeting was in progress. Quickly, I took a seat high in the rear of the hall. The room was about half full of faculty discussing the crisis in the courtyard. No one questioned me, so I just sat and listened.

I sat there for maybe twenty minutes before the professor who had helped me came in. Back in the corridor, he told me he was afraid I had been arrested, but went looking for me after the police left. He led me to a back door opening onto rue Saint-Jacques. A female student was waiting for us at the door. We opened the door a crack and peeked out, saw what looked like hundreds of police, the C.R.S. (Compagnies républicaines de sécurité).

Founded to keep order after World War II, the C.R.S. are the most feared cops in France and they looked the part. Dressed in black battle gear, they carried shields and clubs. Some were armed with machine pistols, the kind you shoot from the hip. Years later, when I saw promos for the movie "Star Wars," Darth Vader reminded me of the C.R.S.

The police seemed to be distracted so the woman and I ran for it. She bolted to the right and I ran the other way, down toward the boulevard Saint-Germain. Policemen shouted, ordering me to stop. I kept running. A few of them chased me, but burdened by all their gear they fell behind. I ran a few blocks then settled into a brisk walk.

Glancing across the street, I spotted a black man I recognized from Black Power meetings. He was a poet and recited his work at the meetings. One of his poems, I remembered, ended with the line, "Whitey say nigger: Cut his throat." I crossed the street and told him what had come down at the Sorbonne and that the police were after me. He took me to his hotel room where we talked for a long time. A serious looking man, he always wore a knit cap with an African design. Finally, I thanked him and headed for the sanctuary of the Right Bank.

At the intersection of the boulevard Saint-Germain and boulevard Saint-Michel, I glanced up Saint-Michel and saw students fighting with police in the street. The air smelled of tear gas. I kept walking down Saint-Germain to the bridge that crosses the Seine to the place de la Concorde.

The next evening I went as usual to the Left Bank in search of a cheap meal. After I left the restaurant, I strolled around watching street entertainers. You could always find groups of people engaged in political debate, too, and I enjoyed listening in, even though my understanding of French was limited.

That night more people than usual were gathering to talk politics and the topic was the events at the Sorbonne the day before. More and more people joined in and soon several groups had become a crowd. Before long, police vans arrived and the crowd, of which I was now a part, moved away, heading toward the boulevard Saint-Michel.

But then the C.R.S. had us surrounded, line after line of them in their "Star Wars" uniforms, with their clubs, shields and guns. What should we do? Speakers urged us on with calls to revolution, or calls to defend the revolution some thought had already begun. Some of us dug up paving stones while others commandeered cars and anything else that could be piled up to form a barricade. We heaved the cars onto their sides, punched holes in the fuel tanks, and drained the gasoline into bottles.

Probably because the crowd had grown so large, the police did not attack until reinforcements arrived. By then the barricades were up and the crowd armed with Molotov cocktails and paving stones. The "Events of May" were on.

For a while the police contented themselves by lobbing tear gas canisters. Housewives threw towels and bed sheets out of their apartment windows. Soaked in water and wrapped around your face, the cloth made a fairly effective gas mask.

At first most of those involved were young, but then older people began to join in. Police attempts to seal off the area leaked and the crowd continued to grow.

When police finally attacked the first barricade, a storm of paving stones and Molotov cocktails kept them at bay. So why were people talking of retreating to the second barricade? It didn't make any sense to me, when the police were having no luck penetrating the first one. But there were tacticians on hand with far more street fighting experience than I had (which was none).

Before we pulled back, the first barricade was soaked with gasoline. Once we were hunkered behind the second barricade, the police stormed over the first one. As they charged into the area between the barricades, a cocktail was thrown onto the first barricade. The police were trapped between a barrage of paving stones and cocktails and the fire behind them.

Night after night the battle raged. Rebel makeshift tactics usually outmaneuvered the police. It seemed the police had to stay within their textbook riot control plans and those plans were no match for their imaginative opponents. Sometimes the frustrated police retreated to formation a distance away and simply watched. Then, as the hour grew late, the crowd would disperse and go home.

In retrospect I wonder if the police had their own agenda. Did the police and military want Charles de Gaulle's government to fall? If they did, they were outmatched on that flank as well. Almost no one knew what de Gaulle was doing, least of all those of us in the streets. Many of us thought we had him reeling, but all the while he was in the Elysée Palace dealing. At the moment when some thought he had fled to his country home at Colombey-les-Deux-Églises, he was secretly flying to Germany to cement the loyalty of his troops stationed there. By the time he returned to Paris, he was on the offensive. More on that later, but for now it seems fair to say that once again de Gaulle's enemies, from whatever side of the political spectrum, had underestimated him. Even at age 77, the man who had rallied France from the depths of its Nazi defeat and restored its national pride was an opponent to be reckoned with.

But before de Gaulle staged his last and in some ways most impressive comeback, the "revolution" spread to other cities and a general strike was called. Workers barricaded themselves inside factories. Most of the country was shut down for weeks. Railroads, subways, buses, all shut down. Vehicles ran out of fuel and many were abandoned on the spot. Unfortunately for their owners, a lot of them became part of the barricades.

During the whole time, the street fighting brawled on night after night. It was almost routine. A crowd would gather on the Left Bank. The police arrived and we went at it until the wee hours.

Then one night, it must have been towards the end of May, the police attacked with a vengeance. We had flung up our barricades near the jardin de Luxembourg. Suddenly the police stormed us from all sides with weapons they hadn't used before, including concussion grenades. One exploded near me, threw me to the ground and left me hard of hearing for days. There were also antipersonnel grenades that exploded on ground contact and sprayed aluminum slivers that ripped into the legs of anyone standing nearby. I escaped that torture, but a German SDS student I knew had his legs sliced up.

That night we were on the run, retreating up the hill to the next barricade and then the next. At the barricade just above Place de la Contrescarpe, on rue de l'Estrapade, we were surrounded and the fighting was intense. We were barely holding off the police assault. A woman was bombing police with pots and pans from her apartment window above. Glancing back, I saw police swarming over the barricade behind us.

I jumped off the wall of cobblestones and noticed a man peering out of an open door. I ran over and he let me in and locked the door behind us. We climbed a flight of stairs to an apartment where about twenty people were hiding out. All of us sat on the living room floor with the lights out. Peeking through the curtains, we saw the remaining battlers taking a terrible beating. It was over.

The strikes continued for a while and the stench of tear gas hung in the air. De Gaulle's government began expelling leftists from other countries. Especially alarming was the deportation of two Spaniards who had fought against Franco in the Spanish Civil War. Both had been awarded France's highest military honor, the Croix de Guerre, for their participation in the liberation of France from Nazi occupation.

As American exiles, we were nervous about our relationship with the government, particularly since another exile group, The Second Front, had publicly called for the overthrow of de Gaulle's government. At least one older American, still in exile from the McCarthy era, was deported to the United States.

I damn near got caught again, simply because I didn't recognize the gravity of the situation. The next afternoon following the last night of fighting I stopped by an apartment where several German SDS students lived. The student with the aluminum shrapnel in his legs was there and the others were nursing him. He was afraid that seeking professional medical attention would lead to his arrest.

I hadn't been there more than a few minutes when the police came knocking at the door. A couple of the guys whisked me into a bedroom and hid me on the package shelf in the closet with boxes piled to conceal me. I hunkered there with my head between my knees for about an hour, until the apartment was silent. The police didn't open the closet door.

Taking a chance that everyone was gone, I pushed the boxes to the floor with a horrifying clatter, climbed off the shelf, lowered myself to the courtyard through the bedroom window and escaped out by the concierge's door. As it turned out, all of the students from the apartment were arrested and deported. Had the police burst into the apartment in the style of a raid, I probably would have been in big trouble.

Over a generation later, what went through my mind on that closet shelf is obscure. But it may well have been one of those times when I asked myself how on earth a guy who started out simply wanting an unjust war to stop, ended up fighting police in Paris.

I was very angry and deeply anguished; I know that ... angry with those responsible for the war in Vietnam, for racism and poverty and other social inequalities. The anguish came from wrestling with just how I was going to deal with my part in it all. How all this took root in me is a long story and probably the best way to tell it is to go back to the beginning.

POWAY, CALIFORNIA   1966

I guess before I go too far back into this story I should get something off my chest. I began working on this book back in 1991, during the Gulf War. In 1996 I picked it up again because I promised my Mom years ago, not long before she died, that my story would be put on paper. 1996 was the year my Dad died and the final impetus to get it done.

Mom saved all the letters we exchanged, as well as the correspondence from my older brother, Ron. She saved newspaper clippings and photographs, too. When she gave me that box of memorabilia, she said, "Here, this is the material you need to write your book. I didn't go through all this for nothing."

I do not relish writing any of this. It has been a long time. The pain of it and most of the memories are still close, incarnate, and as if they are lurking just beneath the surface of my skin, but for my Mom, and so my children might better understand their Dad, I'll tell the story now.

I have always been something of an observer, separating myself from the rest of the crowd to watch and wonder. Why are things the way they are? Why do people do what they do?

As a child in Rutland, Vermont—seven, eight or nine years old—I would pack a lunch in my old army surplus backpack, strap on a canteen full of kool-aid, hop on my bike and head out of town. At the end of Killington Avenue, I would hide my bike in the bushes and hike up the mountain. At the top, I'd find some big rock or log to sit on and look out over the Vermont vista and wonder. Always by myself. Maybe that is the quality I need, the solitude, the watchfulness to help me tell this story.

Since it concluded with little loss of "Allied" life, the Gulf War now seems to have been a lot of thunder about something relatively insignificant. Many expected it to be a longer conflict. However, I am sure that "insignificant" is not the way civilians in Baghdad who were underneath the bombs or western soldiers with some unexplained residual health problem see it.

The lesson in it for me, as someone who struggled so hard in 1967 to understand Lyndon Johnson in the White House and Robert McNamara and his Pentagon, is that young people can still be deluded into fighting and killing and dying, ostensibly for high-minded principles, when in fact we know there was no democracy to protect, nor any danger to U.S. security. It was not a heroic effort. I remember it best from a journalistic photo of what remained after the "Allies" bombed the retreating Iraqi army.

Damn, I don't know, I guess young soldiers will kill and die for a good source of oil. I do remember well the sense of excitement, the pride in wearing my country's army uniform, and the power I felt in becoming accomplished with my sidearm. I remember all of that and more.

But there were so many casualties in Vietnam. At least three million Vietnamese dead, fifty-eight thousand Americans dead, some still missing. How many wrecked bodies? How many so emotionally scarred that they will never heal? So many damaged, in so many ways.

I am writing this at my beach cabin in Saskatchewan. It is February. It is cold. Recalling some of this has pretty much drained me for the moment. I put up a brave front for so many years. I succeeded in much that I've done. I was a good political organizer for Canada's New Democratic Party, managing campaigns all over this country.

But now it is time to admit that I, too, was a casualty of Vietnam. Writing this book at forty–eight years of age (1996) may begin the rebuilding, as a way of dealing with the emotional scars somehow. What if I'd handled my angst differently? Ironically, I turned out to be a lot like the guys who told me their combat stories, full of fear that they hadn't made the grade. No, I didn't kill or torture anybody, but did I let people down?

Now I know that I was so full of fear that I'd let my country and my family down that it did to me what it did to a lot of those Vietnam vets, turned me surly sometimes, sometimes angry, mean and aggressive. Instead of finding peace inside, as I wanted it for my country, I looked for an enemy. My enemy was not the Vietnamese; it was the government of the United States. Looking for the root cause of evil I found it with the capitalists, the military-industrial complex. I was looking for a fight. I was going to prove my manliness. I hated and that hate drove me for years.

I lost myself. All those years of looking for a fight and it spilled into my family life, too. Yet, I honestly thought in many respects that that was how a man should behave.

It all started with the disgust I felt for the kind of behavior, the crap I saw in the Army. I turned it in on myself. Hell, I'm not a chicken: I can be a bad ass, too! That's the way it was and it was such a waste of good people.

Now I weep inside for my peers who really suffered. Some of them have their names on that black wall in Washington. Some are physically wrecked, some emotionally wrecked, some both.

I started school in Rutland, Vermont; kindergarten at Dana School. That's where we lived after moving from Holden, Massachusetts. Holden was where I was born in 1948 and the place we left just before a vicious tornado tore the town apart.

I hated school. I loved to learn, but how I hated school. I rarely studied, which may help to explain why my grades were only average. In my senior year, I got into a co-op program—half a day in school, half on a job. By this time we had moved from Rutland to Springfield, Vermont, back when I was in the fourth grade actually.

I worked for a man named Art Davis, who owned a tile company. I learned ceramic tile setting and some flooring and I helped him with the new house he was building. One day we were up on the roof finishing the chimney and we got into a discussion on Vietnam. We sat on the peak of that fairly steep roof and talked, neglecting our task. Art turned it into a lecture, saying, "Now let me tell you the virtues of the war in Vietnam."

Decades later, I remembered that conversation when with some trepidation I looked Art up before going to my thirtieth high school reunion.

But for the most part my last year of high school was party time, a wonder year for me. We partied from September to June, to say nothing of the summer before. Other than the cars I drove, which I continually bought, sold and traded, I had a project car (the kind of hot rod project I sometimes find myself involved in to this day), a 1940 Ford coupe. For this I rented a garage stall complete with grease pit. I went to the garage a lot, both to get away and to be with the car I loved. The 1940 Ford coupe is still my favorite car.

There was an apartment on the second floor above the garage. The man who lived up there—I knew him as Mr. George— had run a car repair business where I was renting space. He lived up there with his wife and daughter Shirley.

Shirley was twenty-one years old, so when she started hanging out in the garage while I tinkered with the Ford I thought little of it. I enjoyed her company and our talks. We were comfortable with each other.

She worked at Britt's department store at the lunch counter. One evening I stopped in there for a Coke and to say hi. Suddenly the lights went out. We were in the dark of what became known as the great northeast blackout—the one that produced a baby boom nine months later. The store manager hustled the customers out. I still remember how strange it was, as I drove home—no streetlights; storefronts and service stations, darkened.

A few days later I went to the garage after supper and Shirley came down. She looked slimmer than ever in those tight jeans she often wore. I told her I was going over to my older friend Paul Locke's place to do homework. Paul and his wife Jeanne were both working that evening. Would Shirley like to come along?

Shirley watched TV and I pretended to do homework. Then I asked her not to say anything to Jeanne about us being there alone. Paul had slipped me his key earlier and asked me to be discreet. "Oh," she said. "I'll just tell her I watched TV, you did homework, and then we made love."

For several weeks after that, Shirley and I spent a lot of time together. At one of the senior parties at the cottage of somebody's parents near Ludlow, I lost her. I asked everyone if they'd seen her. I went outside and asked again. Somebody pointed up. I looked and there she was, high up on a tree branch, beer in hand. Shirley was a little wild, a freedom echoed in the carefree way she moved, and I loved it. We drove back to Springfield in the season's first snowfall.

Mom was an R.N. working the night shift at the Springfield hospital. With no other place open in the middle of the night, the local cops often stopped by the hospital for coffee. They told Mom I was seeing Shirley.

Mom and Dad sat me down and told me it was inappropriate for me to go with an "older woman." I said I didn't want to stop seeing her so they threatened to take my car away. I couldn't bear the thought of being without my car. That would have been akin to the amputation of a limb, so that was that.

Other cars and girls came and went. In June I graduated from high school with thoughts of California on my mind.

I would have headed to California the day after graduation, but there was the issue of a court date; to deal with a ticket ... the offense was breach of peace by burning tires. Waiting to 'appear' held me up for nearly a week. A small fine and I was gone.

I had been dreaming of living out there for years. My older brother Ron lived with his wife Sandra in a desert town called Poway, just northeast of San Diego. Sandra was a laboratory technician at Scripps Institute in La Jolla while Ron worked on his doctorate at the University of California's La Jolla campus. He chose the school so he could study with Herbert Marcuse, the German-born social and political philosopher who was widely influential during the 1960s. Some accused him of being responsible for much of the student unrest in the United States and Europe. Ron and he became good friends and his influence on Ron was profound.

Ron is my half-brother, actually. His mother died when he was eleven years old. My mother never really accepted him, unfortunately. I remember one summer in the late 1970s, when Ron and I were together at a family reunion in Vermont—my mother's family. My mother gathered us in the back yard of my grandmother's house in Rutland to have a family picture taken and she asked Ron to get out of the photograph.

But I always looked up to my big brother Ron. His influence on me began with my fascination for the political arguments he had with our father when Ron came home to visit from his sales job with Proctor & Gamble before he decided to go to college. Even as a boy, I noticed a lack of reason in Dad's belief that one's opinion ought to be formed by duty, patriotism and respect for authority, rather than real knowledge. Ron might have said that Eisenhower shouldn't have lied about Gary Powers and the U-2 flights over the Soviet Union, while Dad would have countered that unless you knew as much as the president you shouldn't offer an opinion. If Ike thought the spy flights were necessary, then by God it was unpatriotic to question him.

With all that we learned in school about our freedoms and our history of struggling for truth and justice, I was proud to be an American. That was a child's point of view, perhaps, but I put a lot of stock in those teachings. Nevertheless in my teenage years I became more and more uneasy with the unquestioning ways of my Dad and a lot of others, too.

Back in 1961, Ron had left Proctor & Gamble and entered Northwestern University. He got involved in the civil rights movement and ended up joining the protest in Selma, Alabama. Back home in Vermont we watched those civil rights marchers stand up to Jim Clark, the beer-bellied sheriff who personified the ugly image of the American bigot, and we did not know Ron was there.

Then, in the summer of 1963, my sister Nancy and I went to visit Ron in Chicago while our parents traveled to France with Sandra. Our younger brother David got to spend that time with our grandmother in Rutland. Sandra whose real name is Alexandrine, was raised in France. Her Ukrainian father and Czech mother had a small farm outside of Toulouse. My father was born in France and still had family there, although he came to the United States via Quebec as a child just before World War I.

Nancy and I had a wonderful summer. We spent a lot of time at the Evanston beach and several times Ron took us to Wrigley Field to watch the Cubs. He hasn't lived in Chicago since he graduated from Northwestern, but he is still a loyal Cubs fan.

In the evenings, we helped Ron operate his concession at the university's outdoor theater. Ron did it for some much needed cash, but for me those nights were heaven-sent. There was an actress who I thought was surely the most stunningly beautiful and alluring young woman that ever set foot on earth. I was weak in the knees whenever I could steal a look. That was almost forty years ago, when I was fifteen years old. But I still remember her name: Suzie Kuhn.

One evening I took a tray of cold drinks to the dressing room. Suzie was there and I'm sure she had noticed my amorous attention to her charms. She asked me to wash her hair. Wearing only a skirt and bra, she leaned her head over a sink, looked up at me with a coy smile, and said, "Come on, wash my hair." I did and even now my heart races a little as I write this.

Then came a day that probably changed my life. Ron asked Nancy and me if we wanted to go to a civil rights march in downtown Chicago. The Reverend Martin Luther King was to lead the march.

At first I refused to go. Ron said fine, I didn't have to. I may have been testing him, wanting to know if he would let me make my own decision. Anyway, I went, more out of curiosity than anything else.

The crowd was huge and made up mostly of black people (Negro would have been the term of the day). Those were the days before Stokely Carmichael and the Black Power movement. Leading the march, along with Martin Luther King, was the comedian Dick Gregory and activist James Farmer in his trademark overalls.

As we moved through the streets on the way to a lakeside park, the marchers chanted and sang movement songs such as "We Shall Overcome." Intensifying emotion combined with a festive atmosphere and the spiritual music generated a unity more powerful than anything else I have ever experienced.

At the park, we gathered near Buckingham Fountain and listened to speeches. The crowd listened politely until the time neared for King to speak. Then, as the emotion mounted, people began arching on their toes, straining for a glimpse of "the King". Finally King rose up from the throng around the platform. I don't recall a word he said that day, but being there to see and hear that man was a most incredible experience. Though it would be a while before it would have much impact on my life, I think I got the message.

The message was there when I arrived in Poway, too, and I was at least half listening to it. Ron loved to talk politics, especially when our cousin Tim McCarthy came by for a visit. Ron and Tim had pretty much grown up together and they were still close. He had lived with Tim's family when his mother was sick and our father was in the Army and later hospitalized with tuberculosis. When Tim learned that Ron was going to graduate school in California, he quit graduate school at the University of New Hampshire and headed west with Ron to try his hand at writing full-time. His wife Jeannine was working with Sandra at Scripps Clinic. The two couples lived together for the first few months in California, sometimes so broke they had to survive on mussels Sandra and Jeannine gathered at the La Jolla beach during their lunch hour, or rabbits Tim shot in the rocky hills around Poway.

By the time I got there, Tim and Jeannine were renting a small house shadowed by eucalyptus trees, on a rutted road about a mile from Ron and Sandra. So they were together quite often and Ron and Tim would go at it. They were quite a pair: Ron short, slight, with a potbelly, long brown hair and beard; Tim a head taller, slightly stooped, wavy black hair and beard. He paced almost constantly and does to this day—a sign, I think, of some unresolved inner turmoil. They both used their hands a lot when they talked and the more they got into the bourbon at night the faster the hands flew. One of them usually ended up pounding the table. They argued everything from politics to philosophy, Vietnam to the Great Society. Usually I only half-listened, if at all, but I did love what they were doing. There was something about their academic and creative work that really turned my crank. It is an aspect of life I always thought I'd like to get into, but it has never been my métier. I've always worked with my hands, building, fixing cars and houses.

When I first went to California, I landed a good paying job with a tile company, relying on what I had learned with Art Davis during my senior year of high school. I had a letter of reference from him. I walked into a tile company office in nearby Escondido and said I was a tile setter's helper. They hired me on the spot and sent me to a marina in Oceanside where a hotel was going up. Trouble was, the tiling process they used was entirely different from what I had learned. Their process, called deep-set, involved spreading mortar on the wall and applying tiles to it. In Vermont I'd learned the thin-set method of applying tiles to gypsum board with adhesive. So, I had no idea what I was doing.

I was mixing the mortar they referred to as "mud", for about ten tile setters. I busted my butt to keep those guys going. They had to show me everything from scratch.

After the tiles were set it was my responsibility to grout the tile. After a few days of working with mortar and grout my fingers began bleeding. In the last hotel bathroom that I grouted, the blood mixed with the grout producing a lovely pink mixture. I was told to remove it from the wall and start again, but the blood wouldn't stop flowing and the setters told me I better quit before I got fired.

I was ready to quit in any case. The work was so exhausting that it was cutting into the partying. After work, I'd meet a bunch of guys on the beach at La Jolla. We would surf in the evening and then party into the wee hours. Then I'd have to go off and mix mortar and grout tile. I was exhausted. Something had to give and at that time surfing and partying was the most important.

So I got a job in a restaurant kitchen making salads and washing pots. But the Cuban cook was gay and kept hitting on me. He'd do things like drop an ice cube down my shirt as he walked by. I was uncomfortable and didn't know how to deal with him, so I left that job, too.

My next job was at a Hancock service station in Poway. I pumped gas, changed oil, and learned how to do some minor mechanical repairs. It wasn't physically demanding, so I had plenty of energy for partying and enough money to run my '56 Chevy two-door hardtop and date my newfound girlfriend. Her name was Cyndy Tassell. She was slim with wheat-colored hair, not beautiful but darn good looking, and she had the most wonderful touch. Under her touch, I swear I sometimes thought I was in heaven.

That fall Cyndy and I thought we were in trouble. Thinking about marriage we found ourselves in Escondido looking at mobile homes. But it was a false alarm and that was just as well.

I remember the time I went up to Tim's place to borrow his motor scooter. The scooter was their only transportation. He buzzed all over town with Jeannine on the back. They lived about a half-mile up that rutted road. Cyndy lived on a nearby hill and I wanted to take her for a ride on the scooter.

Cyndy's mom was a lovely woman and she liked me a lot. She knew I liked whiskey sours and they had a lime tree in the yard, so, often when I went up there to see Cyndy her mom went out and picked a lime to make me a drink. That was added incentive to visit.

I borrowed Tim's scooter and went tearing up the road to Cyndy's house. There was a sandy stretch of road and the scooter whipped out of control, pitching me over the handlebars. I picked up the scooter, and myself and made it to Cyndy's house. Dirty, with scratched face and bleeding elbows, I told Cyndy's mom I had come to take her daughter for a ride on the scooter. She gave me a look and said, "Forget it."

That was the tenor of my life in those days. In some ways, California was an extension of my last years in high school. Back in Vermont after that summer my sister and I spent with Ron in Chicago, life was again removed from civil rights demonstrations. We watched them on TV news, but I don't believe there was one nonwhite person in Springfield, so it was easy to slip back into the complacency of our middle-class life. I spent a lot of time tinkering with my car and trying to get it on with girls. Most of the time I didn't think much about politics or civil rights.

Then, early in my last year of high school, I met a Baptist minister in North Springfield who was working with a group called Vermont in Mississippi. His name was Phillips Henderson. We spent some time together talking about the side of my life that seemed removed from what interested my friends and immediate family. We didn't talk about religious matters, nor was I particularly religious, but I began attending his services because I respected him for his bravery in voicing an opinion that wasn't too popular at the time.

On children's Sunday that year, in the Reverend Henderson's church, I delivered a sermon and the topic was civil rights. The sermon was my second political act.

Yet, I played out the rest of that year of high school almost oblivious to any strife anywhere. Graduation was a good time, though it's a miracle, with all the road racing and back-seat shenanigans, both mixed with considerable drinking, that I didn't kill myself or become a parent.

Although the escalation of U.S. involvement in Vietnam began with the Tonkin Gulf incident in 1964, I really can't recall an awful lot of discussion on that matter from that time until the summer of 1966. The Vietnam conflict was in the news all right, but it seemed unreal somehow, a little crazy. South Vietnamese governments came and went. A Buddhist monk burned himself to death on a Saigon street. Then some guy torched himself on the steps of a government building in Washington. The Pentagon assured us that everything was under control and the troops would be home soon.

But that awareness (or unawareness) began to change in the California summer and fall of 1966. All my beach buddies and I wanted to do was play with our cars and our girls, drag race and dance, but the damn war just wouldn't go away. We talked about it a little, but not a lot, because discussing it usually ended up in ugly arguments. You didn't want to show too much misgiving about the war because someone sure as hell would question either your patriotism or your manhood. But I thought for lots of people the question of U.S. involvement had little to do with anything rational.

Sure, my main reason for being in California was to have fun in the surf-and-hot-rod culture, but there were other snippets of experience that shook me out of my social amnesia.

One involved a horrendous camping trip Ron and Sandra, Tim and Jeannine and this reluctant passenger took that summer. It was on the Fourth of July weekend, not long after I arrived in California. We all piled into Ron's little Volvo, five adults and two dogs, one of them a huge German Shepard named Erich, and headed—where else—deeper into the high summer desert to Joshua Tree National Monument. The car did not have air-conditioning and as we left the ocean breezes behind the air rushing into the car turned so hot we had to ride with the windows up. We were crammed into a mobile sweatbox and I remember thinking that we had to be crazy to put ourselves through such an

23

ordeal. Tim was the only one who seemed to enjoy it, or at least tolerate it without bitching. Of course the trip was his idea so he may have been saving face.

Earlier, though, in the somewhat cooler mountains east of Poway, we drove through the town of Ramona. Demonstrators milled outside the little courthouse, which looked like part of the set of a western movie. Ron and Tim said a man was being tried on charges resulting from his efforts to organize farm workers. His name was Cesar Chavez. I think that was the first time he was put on trial in his long battle to form the United Farm Workers union. Ron and Tim attended some of the trial.

From then on, I started paying attention whenever I saw workers in a field. Lots of them were kids. They lived in shacks most Americans would feel guilty about housing their dog in.

Years later, here in Saskatchewan, some political colleagues and I had lunch with Cesar. By then he was a hero to me. He was on a North American tour promoting the UFW grape boycott and I was pleased to find that I liked him (unlike some of the other luminaries I have met). He seemed warm and genuine, a physically small man with an almost shy smile who made a big difference in the lives of a lot of people.

Anyway, Ramona was the high point of that weekend for me. We stopped at the Salton Sea and I plunged into the water only to discover that it was hot! Everything was hot that weekend. At Joshua Tree, we spread a blanket, sat down and drank hot tequila with salt and lime. Tim's theory was that at that time of year we would have the place pretty much to ourselves. He got that right. There was only one other group, as I recall. That night we bedded down on the ground and the moon was so bright we couldn't sleep. For me, it was a weekend from hell. But one that I remember.

By the end of that year, Sandra was plainly pregnant and expecting the baby in the spring. I began to get the feeling that my welcome was wearing thin, although we got along most of the time. Ron got up early and after he took Sandra and Jeannine to work, a chore he alternated with Tim, he would study through the day. Sandra would come home and cook one of her fabulous meals. She was a strong-looking woman of medium height, with Slavic features and short brown hair. Her English was fluent and precise, but she spoke it with a marked accent and a cadence from another culture. Her Ukrainian father was working in Kerensky's government before the Bolsheviks seized power during the revolution of November 1917. His girlfriend was a Bolshevik and she told him he was on a hit list and he'd better get out. So he fled to Prague and it was in the newly formed Czechoslovakia where he met Sandra's mother.

Sandra and Jeannine were quite a pair. They drew close in what must have been an expatriate alliance—two women who to some degree were still making their way in a new land, with American husbands who were hardly more than boys to them in some ways. Jeannine was petite, pretty, her brown hair dyed blonde, a real sweetheart I thought. She always struck me as tender, vulnerable. I remember loving the way she called Tim "Tee-mo-tey."

Then came New Year's Eve. The four of them drove down to Tijuana to celebrate. I brought Cyndy to the house and left my car in the carport behind the house where Ron always parked. Tim said Ron drank too much that night. Anyway, they came home much earlier than I had expected and there was my car in Ron's spot. I was in the bedroom with Cyndy. Ron stormed into the house cussing and castigating "that goddamn Dick." That was it. I took Cyndy home, came back, loaded my stuff into the car and left.

I moved in with a guy I knew. It was a dumpy little place and I thought, "Well, this is the pits." What should I do? The possibility of being drafted was on my mind. After going to see Ron and patching things up, I decided to head back east. I came to some kind of awkward understanding with Cyndy, too.

It turned out to be an interesting trip. But as I nosed the Chevy out of Poway at about noon that January day in 1967, I was oblivious to a future that was already coming to meet me. History was probing my life in ways I was far from imagining and soon it would have a hold on me that I have never been able to shake off.

FORT GORDON, GEORGIA
1967

Vermont was my destination that winter, but along the way I was already seeing things a little differently than I had heading west the summer before. That first day on the road was when I started noticing the migrant worker camps. They actually lived in derelict cars with clotheslines strung from car to car.

Tucson was as far as I got that day. The next night I made it to Texas. I was trying to get as far as Dallas, but I was too tired. I pulled off the highway into a small community called Roscoe. The place had the feel of a ghost town. Tumbleweed was blowing down the street. I stopped, looked east down the main street and saw a pink motel sign. For about eight bucks I got a room with an old steel bed and a primitive shower. There was no stall or tub. You simply stood over a drain in the floor and pulled the chain. Water cascaded from a showerhead that looked like a sunflower. The bed was a back buster.

Further east—I think it was in Tennessee—I saw kids running around with no shoes on. It was a mild January day by Vermont standard, but still only about 40 degrees, cold enough if your family couldn't afford to buy you shoes. Some of their shacks were moored on the murky river.

Cops were following me almost constantly. I'd leave one jurisdiction and another cop would get on my tail. Though I wasn't pulled over, it was scary because I didn't know what they were up to.

Anyway, I ended up stopping in New Jersey to see a girl named Sherry Statham. Her family had a camp (that's what

Vermonters call a cottage) on the same lake where my folks had theirs. We were driving around Hawthorne that evening when the cops pulled us over. They asked to see my registration. Then they told us to get out of the car and they radioed for a tow truck. They said they had a report of a stolen Chevrolet from California and they thought there was something irregular about my registration. My car was towed to a police compound and the cops took us to the station.

The police station looked like the set for some TV show, complete with the desk sergeant perched above us. I was arguing that there was nothing irregular about my registration and started to lose my cool. Sherry tried to calm me down. But I was yelling at the sergeant, shouting that I wanted my car back. That '56 Chevy was my baby. I washed it every day, waxed it once a week. Sherry kept urging me to calm down. She said her Mom knew the police chief. Finally she got hold of her Mom and things were straightened out pretty fast. But it was a lesson to me that they were able to take my car and impound it for no good reason.

Back in Vermont, I felt pressured to make some decisions before the draft board made them for me. It was too late to enter college that winter and I was prime picking for the draft. I considered finding temporary employment with plans to enter school that fall. But, given the ongoing escalation of the war, it seemed doubtful I would have remained undrafted until September.

I was uncomfortable with the war, but not enough to give any thought to avoiding service because of that. Someone told me that if I enlisted in the Army for a three-year stint I would have a choice of vocation. I checked it out with the recruitment office in Rutland and found it to be true. Being a tank mechanic sounded a hell of a lot better than being drafted into the infantry. And later I could take that skill back to civilian life.

I also felt a need to please my father. Dad and Mom hadn't been happy when I took off to go surfing in California instead of going to college. Dad loved to talk about his Army experiences and I sensed that he had always felt inadequate because he got sick while training as a medic and was given a medical discharge.

But I sure didn't want to be part of the killing and dying in Southeast Asia. Too many people I respected were saying it was wrong, that horror called the war in Vietnam. And they had reasons that made sense. Others talked about patriotism and defending the greatest country in the world. At the time I found something attractive in all the arguments and the upshot was that I enlisted.

So, on January 23, 1967, about seven months after graduating from high school, I was inducted into the U.S. Army, in Manchester, New Hampshire. We were the usual ragtag bunch of recruits, some skinny, some fat, most of us just out of high school, still kids, really, and a long way from the John Wayne type of soldier we saw in the movies. Anyone who has served in the military will find my first weeks in the Army depressingly familiar.

As we traveled south to our processing center at Fort Jackson, South Carolina, I tried to talk with the others about what we might expect in basic training and about Vietnam. We had been treated with respect by recruiters and other handlers to that point. We were now part of a respectable, mature organization and were headed for training that would qualify us to help defend our country. It was heady stuff. But Vietnam? Had you placed a map of the world in front of those guys, most of them couldn't have found the place.

Screaming corporals greeted us as we piled off the bus at the process center. They called us a bunch of useless pussies whose station in life wasn't worth a fuck. It didn't take long for the military's well-known system of tearing you down then rebuilding you as fuel for the fighting machine to kick in. Some of us balked. Those that did got to know the nuance of the push-up real fast. I had the good sense to keep my mouth shut as I observed the Army's method with incredulity.

Over the next several days we were given medical exams and issued our uniforms, boots, shoes and a duffel bag to put it all in. And of course we lost our hair to butcher barbers who had wide smiles of enjoyment, the kind of smile some nurses have when they are about to give you a shot. We also took a battery of tests, the kind they give you in elementary school to determine IQ and aptitude.

Then one morning I was called away and told to report to a nearby office. It felt good to escape the corporals' abuse and harassment. But I was nervous about what might be up.

There was no need to worry. The officer I reported to greeted me with the same respect as the recruiter back in Rutland: "Hello, Private Perrin. Please be seated." Please be seated? Where I had just come from I would have been told to seat my sorry ass on the fucking chair. The officer told me that I had done well on the tests and the Army wanted me to attend Officer Candidate School. I said I would think it over.

Other officers made the same proposal two more times before I finished basic training. Each time I said no. If I ended up fighting, killing and maybe even dying, that was one thing. But to order others to do it in Vietnam? To me, Vietnam was not Normandy. How could I have ordered men to risk their lives for such dubious reasons? My decision not to become an officer was political. But later, as the end of basic training neared I found myself frustrated with that decision because I was enjoying the military structure more. I thought seriously that if it were not for the Vietnam fiasco I might have looked at an Army career as an officer. Without Vietnam, I probably wouldn't have had the offer.

After a couple of weeks at the Fort Jackson processing center we were shipped to Fort Gordon, Georgia for Basic Infantry Training. Fort Gordon is located near Augusta.

A few weeks into training another lesson in military politics came in our barracks one evening when I was practicing bayonet drill with a broom. Steve Reeves, a recruit from New Hampshire, grabbed another broom and challenged me to a duel. He was bigger than me and closing in fast. I dropped my broom trying to avoid him. We hit the floor with Steve on top and the brooms tangled between us. The impact knocked the breath out of me, left me gasping for air. Steve was screaming. He had broken a leg.

When the drill sergeant arrived, I started to explain what had happened. Our squad leader interrupted me. To protect me, he explained that Steve had fallen out of his bunk. Steve ended up with his leg in a cast and had to start basic training all over again after the bone healed.

Those eight weeks of basic training at Fort Gordon were better than I had expected. I had a sense of accomplishment. My body was stronger and I became more coordinated. I grew to love the rhythm of the group march, the graceful feeling of short order drill, getting tighter as a unit day by day, physically, emotionally. Even the drill sergeants began treating us more like human beings.

That part of it made me feel good, but there was always the ugliness, too. There was one black guy, for example, who didn't think this was his Army. He openly balked and shirked, causing all of us in the company much grief. Sometimes he would slow us down or otherwise create situations that would cause us to be reprimanded or punished. Then one night a group of guys gave him a "blanket party". They edged up to his bunk while he slept, held him defenseless under his blanket, beat the hell out of him then told him to get with the drill.

He never did. One day he disappeared and the Army never gave any explanation. I didn't understand him then. I was displeased with him, too. I couldn't fathom the depth of his frustration, disillusionment, anger, disenfranchisement. I wish I could talk with him now.

Another guy disappeared from basic training as well. One evening in the barracks before lights out we heard people yelling from the floor below. This was no bellowing drill sergeant, but rather cries of distress and alarm. I ran down. The commotion was in the latrine. I looked in and saw blood running down the wall and yet more spurting from the wrist of a GI convulsing on the floor. An ambulance came and took him away. His fate was never disclosed to the rest of us.

Then there were the guys who stuck it through but simply didn't fit in. The guy bunking above me, for example, was slight, effeminate, physically weak. His name was Paul Pavone. In military or physical things, he botched nearly everything he did or touched, but in one sense he was a godsend because his performance next to mine made for a rather flattering comparison. He was aiming for a medical discharge because of a weak heart.

But Paul was tidy and made a nice tight bunk. His belt buckle glittered and there was nothing out of place in his locker. He helped me achieve those perfect hospital corners on my bunk.

Sometimes during marches and runs Paul would stumble and fall. The nearest drill sergeant would kick him back to his feet. The poor guy shouldn't have been there. I hope he got his discharge and went back to modeling clothes.

Everywhere we marched or ran, we chanted. (I especially enjoyed the "airborne shuffle," a pace halfway between march and run. Some chants were fun: "Ain't no use in lookin' down, ain't no discharge on the ground"; some were crude: "I don't know but I been told, Eskimo pussy's mighty cold"; some were designed to instill hatred for the enemy: "I wanna be an airborne ranger, I wanna go to Vietnam, I wanna kill a Viet Cong," over and over and over.

Soon some guys were getting tattoos proclaiming "death before dishonor." Those walking works of art were guys from small-town New England. With bravado seething from their pores, they were unrecognizable from the quiet bunch on the bus nine weeks earlier. Still recognizable, though, was their almost total lack of knowledge about Vietnam issues, the history and politics, and most still could not have pointed to Vietnam on a world map.

Of course most recruits were somewhere between the misfits and the Rambos. On occasion, I'd try to talk with some of the others about Vietnam. Generally, they simply didn't want to discuss it. I think most of them were hoping it would go away.

It wouldn't go away for me, though. Toward the end of basic training, we were allowed more free time in the evenings and one weekend pass. I began meeting soldiers who had returned from Vietnam. With stiff upper lips, they'd say, "It's tough over there." But put a few beers in their bellies and the stories poured out.

As they told their stories, you could watch them turn surly, aggressive, angry. They were kind of scary, a little spooky. It has taken me years to understand where that comes from in a man. The source, it seems to me, is fear, being downright scared. Maybe it is the fear of knowing what kinds of ugliness you are capable of, maybe the fear that you are losing control of a situation.

Meanwhile, basic training went on. There was a long march into the field, where we were supposed to bivouac and put into practice much of what we had been learning in the weeks before. It was raining. And it kept raining. We pitched our tents in the rain. Everything we did was scrutinized and timed. I remember standing in a breakfast chow line with my tray, edging along in the rain as they slopped food onto the tray. I went to sit with my back against a tree. The eggs on my tray were floating in rainwater. By the second night, my sleeping bag was drenched.

A nighttime infiltration course culminated our basic training. We hunched in a trench while machine guns played fire overhead. On cue, we lunged out of the trench and crawled underneath barbed wire, the live rounds whizzing in the darkness above us, explosive charges blasting on every side to imitate mines and mortars. The object was to crawl through the course, past the machine guns then charge some straw dummies and bayonet them. Our performance was timed. Either you moved your ass or the drill sergeant's wrath was upon you. On my back under the barbed wire, working my way around one of the explosive bunkers, tracer bullets flaring above, I bumped into another soldier's boots. Evidently, fear had petrified him. There was no room to crawl around him and I yelled at him to get going. He kept screaming that he couldn't. Thinking of the sergeant with the stopwatch, I unsheathed my bayonet and gave him a good poke. He still wouldn't move. Generally I empathized, but that time my fear of the drill sergeant ruled. I ended up crawling over him. Later, when the lights came on, he was still there, terrified.

Happily, the weekend pass toward the end of basic training was a lighter time. Several of us spent it in Atlanta. We found a guy old enough to rent a car, drove from Fort Gordon to Atlanta on Saturday afternoon and checked into a hotel near Peachtree Street. Then we bought enough beer and ice to fill the bathtub and had the makings of a party.

After a few beers, we headed out for a bite to eat. In the lobby, some guy asked if we wanted dates. Hell, yes! We gave him our room number and he said he would send the girls up right away. So, thinking he was a right fine southern gentleman who saw we were soldiers and wanted to help us out in appreciation for our service, we trooped back to the room. How naïve can you get? These are the kinds of kids governments send off to war.

The girls arrived and we all had a couple more beers. Imagine how shocked we were when our "dates" demanded their fees up front. With all of our cash combined, we couldn't have paid for even one of those hookers. They threatened to sic guys on us who would do us grievous bodily harm, then hustled out of our room. We went out for the rest of the evening, partly to make ourselves scarce, and ended up having a hell of a time in a topless bar. Distracted by the delights of the place, we ran up more of a tab than we could afford and had to sneak out.

Natural justice caught up with me early Monday morning when, severely weakened by all that alcohol, I had to complete the daily run before breakfast. I thought I was going to die, which reminds me of another time in basic training when I became quite ill.

One evening after training, I was so weak I had to climb the barracks stairs on my hands and knees. I guess I had an ear infection and fever. I didn't want to show any weakness and I sure didn't want to go on sick call. That was a hassle to be avoided. They made you pack up all your gear into the duffel bag and report to company headquarters where plenty of humiliation was dished out. So I phoned my nurse mother and she mailed me some antibiotics that cured me.

I knew I could count on Mom to take care of things like that, but I always had an uneasy relationship with her, usually respectful but never close. I'm not sure why. Maybe it was because Dad and I bonded more. Dad had a patriarchal, old-world way of treating Mom. She tolerated him. But kids, it seems, take sides and I took his.

Before I finish telling about my time at Fort Gordon, I should mention that my finest hour as a soldier came during my time there. One day we were called to inspection at guard mount. An officer moved up and down our files, stopping at each soldier, inspecting uniforms and weapons and quizzing us on military knowledge. He chose me as the outstanding soldier at guard mount, which got me out of the Saturday morning barracks inspection. I got to be the colonel's orderly instead—a much pleasanter way to spend a Saturday morning.

And I even got a letter signed by the commander, Colonel Richard Kerr. "Having been selected from a large group of your fellow soldiers is truly an honor, particularly in this early stage of your Army service," the letter said.

Man, did I feel on top of the world that day. And wouldn't my Dad be proud! The letter confirmed for me so much of what I had been brought up to value: pride, honor and fulfillment of duty. A young man wants to fit in some place, to be a person valued by his parents, elders and peers. Such an enormous struggle it was to experience a profound face-off between the values of what I considered my manly duties and the other values I thought one should embrace, values such as compassion and understanding. Shouldn't there be a damn good reason to allow oneself to be sent off to a distant land to kill people?

With the end of basic training upon us, the draftees in our cycle were getting uneasy about where the Army would send them next. Clerical school? Not likely and they knew it. When orders were finally posted on the company bulletin board, you could tell which guys were headed for advanced infantry training by the stunned looks on their faces. I was headed for wheeled vehicle mechanical training at Fort Leonard Wood, Missouri, the next square on my hopscotch into the history of a nation at war in Vietnam, but also at war with itself.

FORT LEONARD WOOD,
MISSOURI 1967

The next square landed me at Fort Leonard Wood for wheeled vehicle mechanical training, which was required before advancing on to track vehicles. I was flown there via Fort Polk, Louisiana, where several guys were dropped off for advanced infantry training. They were a pretty somber bunch.

I was wondering if the abusive ways of basic training would continue and was pleased to find the atmosphere a bit more civil at Leonard Wood. Civility isn't something you find a lot of in the Army, but after a few weeks the relative calm in me was shattered.

For the first several weeks of training I was able to wipe out questions about Vietnam and concentrate on my studies. I worked diligently and was always near or at the top of my class.

Then one day a bunch of us went to the enlisted men's club and overheard some guys bragging about torturing Vietnamese people. Of course the torturers didn't regard them as people; they were "gooks." How else could you live with yourself?

At about the same time rioting broke out in Detroit and Newark. American soldiers were called out to suppress American people (not for the first time, by any means). How can a soldier turn a gun on his own people? It seemed to me then that you can do it the same way you can torture gooks—by regarding those people as lesser beings, in this case "niggers."

Racism troubled me, at least since that march in Chicago, when I heard Martin Luther King speak. The Army said it wouldn't tolerate racism, but it sure looked to me like the Army found it a useful tool for manipulating soldiers. When Vietnam commander General William Westmoreland spoke about the war, we saw a gentleman soldier. But scratch the surface of the organization he led and it was very ugly.

Still, the guys I trained with talked of other things. Fast cars and fast girls topped the list. One guy's girlfriend even mailed him a pair of her unwashed panties. He would lie on his bunk in the evening with the panties draped over his face, of course to a chorus of laughter.

Those weeks also put a strain on my relationship with my brother Ron. That was hard, at least for me, because we corresponded a lot. I wrote to him regarding my continuing confusion about our role in Vietnam. He responded with a scathing critique of U.S. foreign policy. I read it as a betrayal of his country and, as I think about it now, I suppose I took it as a criticism of me for participating. Anyway, I remember thinking Ron was overreacting and if he didn't damn well know that he lived in the best country in the world, then he might even be nuts. I wrote home and told Mom and Dad I thought my brother was crazy. Here are some excerpts from those letters, Ron's first. It is dated 6 April (1967):

> With Russia and China at each other's throats and with Ho Chi Minh continuing to refuse Mao's offer of Chinese troops it seems obvious to me that there is no such thing as a worldwide communist conspiracy with one united leadership. What there is, is a rising tide of revolution and hope in much of the world, a hope of the poor and starving and the exploited that they might finally begin to enjoy some of the benefits of the 20th century. For some reason, which is not yet clear to me, although I hope to clarify it in my article on anticommunism, the United States supports the government in power and ignores the desires and dreams of the people. In so doing the U.S. assumes the role of the capitalist power which Karl Marx predicted would stand against the people of the world who did not own land, or businesses or share in the wealth of their countries. And so the leaders of the revolutions in these countries look to Marxist doctrine to try and understand their situation and get the rich off their backs. To that extent they are communists but because they are different men in different countries with different pasts the only thing they share is a hatred for America. If they are Vietnamese they distrust China

because the Vietnamese have fought the Chinese for 2,000 years and no man, whether he is Karl Marx or Lyndon Johnson, is going to make that hatred and mistrust disappear. The most he can do, if he is Johnson, is force the Vietnamese to ask for Chinese help and the fact that all our bombing of the north has not done that shows how reluctant Ho Chi Minh is to bring China into his country. In other words there will not be a worldwide and single-minded communist bloc unless we make it!

As for the question of who asked us to stop communism it is obvious that it was not the English, or the French or the Japanese or a lot of other people. The South Koreans are there in Vietnam but their government is a military dictatorship supported by us just as the Saigon government is. Did you know that we pay the salaries of those South Korean troops? I didn't until a week ago when someone phoned CBS and asked them and CBS said, "But of course." The fact is that only those men, in Southeast Asia and the U.S., who stand to lose a lot of money if the people win, asked us to stop communism.

The only reason I'm saying all of this Dick is that your head is in a noose and I think you should know what the rope is made of. Whether or not that helps is for you to tell me....

In that same letter, Ron urged me to tell my family about the tales of torture I had passed on to him. He wrote, "Letters we get from Betty [my mother] sound as if you were in some kind of Boy Scout camp. She speaks of how you were able to keep the windows open at night, or of your earaches and how pleased she is that you were able to take pride in the inspection awards your platoon earned. I don't want to speak against her but I have to tell you that the letters sickened me because I knew what you were really doing there, learning to kill or be killed...."

But instead of telling my Mom about the stories of torture I had heard, this is part of what I wrote to her April 16, 1967. I was in the PX cafeteria drinking coffee and writing letters. The whole situation left me so emotional that my handwriting was shaky:

Now that Dad is gone for a while I think I can say some things about Ron and what is happening in Poway. To say it bluntly I'm beginning to think he is a little off his rocker. Somehow he believes that this society is all screwed up and that a government based on Marxist doctrine will one

37

day take over as the U.S. government. When he had friends in his house he talked about "the Revolution." He and his friends believe that someday the U.S. government will be overthrown by this small minority and that we will then be under Marxist Communism. He continuously talks about the evils of capitalism and our free enterprise. Undoubtedly our system is imperfect but it is the best that exists. When Sasha [Ron's son] becomes 18 he [Ron] plans to move to another country so that he [Sasha] will not be drafted. Living with him for some time, he managed to get me turned in this direction. I'm not saying that I think everything this country does is perfect. I think even you will agree with me on this point. Someday I'll let you see the letter I got from him last week. I wasn't sure before but I believe something has to be wrong with a person that thinks like him. I met quite a few of his friends and from the way they talked I got the impression that those people have been rejected by our society and in retaliation they are rejecting our society. I've also found that those people are a very small minority very much shunned by most college students.

I don't think it wise that Dad know this about Ron because I think it's important for him to be proud of his son, getting his Master's, etc. I'm telling you this so you can protect Nancy and David [my siblings] from it. You don't know how close I came to accepting Ron's ideas. If Nancy and David are to accept principles like Ron's they should come to find it on their own. I was subjected to seven months of brainwashing and it came close to working. Ron's objective, I believe, was to use me as another person just to expand his principles. He urges me in his letter to write home and say things against the U.S. and its policies. Just as a means of trying to spread his ideas.

As I said before many of his thoughts I agree with, but when he puts them together as an end they seem to be the ideas of a maniac.

These things are hard to say about someone you love and I've tried to push them back in my mind and just realize his good points. Maybe you find these things hard to believe but you haven't lived with him and had these things pressed into you...

That letter is written on stationary with a big logo in the upper left-hand corner. It depicts a squad of soldiers charging out of a helicopter. The letter certainly indicates the intensity of the struggle in my mind. And rereading what I wrote might well have prompted me to consider again some of my family relationships.

I feared my father, no two ways about it. His idea of a good father was based on a model of complete, unbending control. It was the "Because I said so!" school of parenting. When he felt his control slipping, he would spin into a verbal rage.

He measured the success of other men by the amount of control they had. He looked up to his younger brother, my Uncle Marcel, because Marcel had men working "under him." Marcel owned a granite sandblasting business in Barre, Vermont, a town with a worldwide reputation in the industry that drew granite workers, some of them highly skilled, from Quebec, France and Italy. A heart attack killed him one morning in 1969 just as he was opening his office door.

Dad never had more than one man "under him" at the barbershop. But he did have his wife and kids.

I was Dad's favored child. He took me hunting and fishing. We built things together out at the family camp on Lake Hortonia. I busted my butt to protect that relationship. From the time I was eleven years old until I left home at eighteen he relied on me to shovel the snow and mow the lawn. When he came in from work, I made sure the rock-and-roll on the stereo was turned off. Sometimes I got him his slippers and brought him his jug of wine.

By then, I knew well how far I could push him and was careful not to go any further. I knew all his buttons; I sensed the threshold that led to rage. It wasn't unlike the kind of relationship you might cultivate with a drill sergeant. But the times Dad and I spent alone together were always good.

My father was a good man in many ways. He was honest and hard working. But he never learned how to control his own temperament very well. When he was in a good mood, he was totally charming. Other family members have said that in all those aspects—the charm, the temper, the unbending control—he was much like his own father, Marius.

Mom, Ron and my sister Nancy were not as eager to dance his dance. All three of them, without much of a relationship to protect, sometimes with delight, pushed him until he pitched over the edge. David, the youngest and the closest to Mom, was traumatically terrorized by Dad.

When Dave was about six years old, Mom, recognizing that he needed protection, put her foot down and told Dad to lay off, or else. And he did. He was, relatively speaking, mellower from then on.

The easiest way for me to deal with this family schism was to stay a safe distance from anything that caused Dad consternation. Mom and I were not close and I avoided Nancy. Ron was long gone and not part of the daily family dynamic.

Our family organization, then, was a lot like society as a whole. Power was concentrated at the top while those below struggled for a place. Adversarial relationships were inevitable. But those old ways of relating to one another don't cut it any more. Not in our families and not in our politics. It took me two failed marriages and a lot of other damaged relationships to realize that.

As a parent to my three kids, Shayne, Ashley and Greg, I was at times almost as rigid as my Dad. From time to time, though, I was able to let go some, and experienced a reasoned relationship with them instead of having them toe the line because they feared me.

I resolved before Shayne was born that I would not employ any method of corporal punishment on my kids. I remembered feeling terror when my Dad came after me with a strap, and so I kept to that resolve.

So why not build healthy relationships at all levels—from the family to a really new world order? Healthy relationships are built by people employing principles of equality, cooperation and collaboration. Fault lies with those who have an unhealthy need to control power and wealth, and fault lies, too, with those of us who allow this to go on.

But, hardly more than a kid myself, I was far from realizing any of that during those eight weeks at Fort Leonard Wood. One night toward the end of that training I went to the base movie theater alone. After the feature film, they showed a short propaganda piece designed to inspire patriotism in the soldiers who sat through it. There were shots of some of America's most spectacular scenery—the Grand Canyon, the Rocky Mountains, Mount Rushmore, the Statue of Liberty, stuff like that. At the end, jet fighters screamed across a sky of pristine blue.

The film moved me, but not in the way the Army intended. As I was walking back to my barracks, I was suddenly overwhelmed and started crying. I headed for a secluded wooded area, sat down under a tree in the dark and bawled my heart out. How could such a beautiful country be going so wrong?

That night was another turning point, one of those thunderbolts that stop your life in its tracks, illuminate the possibility of another way. Sitting there in the dark, under a tree at Fort Leonard Wood, Missouri, I was determined to find out what in the world was going on. And why.

FORT SILL, OKLAHOMA   1967

With two weeks leave coming at the end of the Fort Leonard Wood training program, I made plans to spend a week with Mom and Dad in Vermont and a week with Ron, Sandra and their new son Sasha in California.

Back home, I found a growing rift between my folks and Ron—a rift caused in large measure by the different messages I sent—and I felt like I was walking a tightrope across a deep chasm. I wanted my parents to know that I had been doing well with the Army training and, most important to me, I wanted them to know I was tough enough, mature enough to "take it." Ron and I, by mail, on the other hand, discussed political and social issues as they related to the war in Vietnam.

In Vermont, the family skirted the Vietnam question until the evening before I was scheduled to fly out to California. At the supper table, I simply told Mom and Dad that I disagreed with what was happening in Vietnam, but that if ordered to go, despite my belief that there was no value in that war effort, I would go. They later said they couldn't recall that comment.

There was more discussion in the Springfield community about the pros and cons of the war than there had been the last time I was there. Most of the people I talked with were in favor of the U.S. involvement. I remember some of the comments I heard when I expressed my misgivings: "Why are you so concerned about soldiers dying in Vietnam when more people are killed every year in traffic accidents?" "You should just mind your own business and do as you're told, because the President knows a lot more than you do—if you had the information he has, then you'd have a right to judge the issue." "Well, Dick, our soldiers may be doing ugly things, but the communists are doing uglier things."

Clearly, those people were simply making excuses and they didn't know much about what was going on in Vietnam. To me, the notion that it was not my place to question authority contradicted the very foundation of democracy. And I had learned in high school history classes (history and social studies were the two courses that grabbed me) that one of the lessons of the Nuremburg trials after World War II was that pleading "I was just following orders" was not an acceptable defense.

I needed to please, especially my father, and I needed to appease my conscience. That dichotomy was tearing me apart.

In California, Ron was careful not to raise the Vietnam issue. I brought it up, but I felt it was something I needed to resolve for myself. Ron made his position clear, including his concern for my well-being.

A high school buddy, Tim Closson, who was living in Ventura, came to Poway for a visit toward the end of that week. On my last evening there, we went with Ron down to Tijuana and had ourselves a time.

Saying goodbye the next day was emotional. There was no mention of Vietnam. But at least I knew that Ron still cared about me, even though I was in the military he had come to oppose so deeply. After those last hugs, Tim and I climbed into his hotrod and he drove me to the airport in L.A. I didn't see Tim again until he showed up one day in my bathroom in Saskatchewan while I was sitting in the tub and he told me he was AWOL from the Army. But more of that later.

I had orders to report to Fort Sill, Oklahoma, the next day and intended to go on military standby and catch a flight out of LAX. But the state universities had just finished up for the year and the airport was swarming with homeward bound students. There were no seats available.

With no possibility of reaching Fort Sill within 24 hours, I reported to the Shore Patrol office at the airport. They arrested me on the spot. I pleaded that I wasn't AWOL, had no intention of going AWOL, and would have been able to get to Oklahoma in plenty of time if there had been an open seat. "Too bad," they said.

"If you can't get there by tomorrow, you're AWOL." Then they put me in a cell.

The next morning they drove me to the bus terminal and I headed out by bus. By the time I reached Fort Sill, I was about forty-eight hours late and received a verbal reprimand. But there were no other consequences.

A letter I wrote to my folks shortly after I made it to Fort Sill pretty well sums up how torn and confused I was at the time. The letter was dated June 21, 1967:

> Dear Folks,
>
> I finally made it here about noon Monday. They gave me no trouble at all when I got here.
>
> The fort is a lot better than Leonard Wood. We have nice big barracks with ceramic tile bath, tile floors and huge porches in front. My only complaint is the heat. It gets about 100 degrees in the afternoon. Also, we don't get the harassment we got at Leonard Wood.
>
> Thank you very much for the great week at home. Home cooked meals, a nice bed, and the family around seemed like being in heaven. I hope I can go back home again soon.
>
> During my four days with Ron, we did a lot of talking. I must say that he has become much more conservative since I saw him last. Many of the things I wrote in that letter from Fort Wood are just not true of him. I believe him to be a man very interested in the future of this country and of the world. Ron loves his country just as I do and wants good to come from living in it. He wants very much for Sasha to grow up in a world without prejudice and hate. We still have our differences, but we still agree on the majority of situations that exist in the world. For instance the war in Vietnam. I've been in the Army for five months and I still think our government is making a big mistake. I am proud to wear the uniform of the U.S. but if the time comes when I have to go to Vietnam it will be hard to directly support something I feel is morally wrong...

I started the track vehicle mechanics course and again I did well. I was determined to give it my best, but I was also determined to find out all I could about what was happening in Vietnam. I searched bookstores and the library for anything related to the history of Southeast Asia. Those books taught me that the Vietnamese had been at war for a long time, first against China, then France, the Japanese during World War II, then France again, and finally the United States.

After lights out, I would sit on a can in the latrine and read for hours. Night after night, I read. It became clear to me that not only was it wrong for the United States to put young men into a position of committing unspeakable acts against the Vietnamese, but that from the beginning the U.S. involvement in Southeast Asia was politically misdirected.

Despite that new conviction, I was torn between a sense of duty and the realization that without a doubt the war was morally and politically wrong. God, how I wanted to be a proud, brave, patriotic soldier. I didn't want to be considered a coward.

I tried to talk with other soldiers, but the usual response was along the lines of, "Yeah, you're probably right, Dick. I just don't want to hear about it. I just want to get all this over with and go back home." They were a good bunch of guys and, ironically enough, I was selected to be their squad leader. Some of them warned me I better be careful or I might get in trouble.

The hearts and minds of the GIs in my squad had not been won over to the war cause any more than the hearts and minds of the Vietnamese peasants herded into strategic hamlets. Still, I was willing to listen to proponents of the war, hoping I would hear something convincing. I asked the instructors and a couple of officers at the school what they thought about it. I went to see the chaplain to talk about it. He said that things he disagreed with came across his desk all the time, but he simply fulfilled his obligations without question. He was a little less than inspiring.

I phoned Ron, told him what I was up to and mentioned that I sure wished there were other soldiers around that I could talk to. He said he had just read about a soldier at Fort Sill who had been in trouble because of his antiwar views. His name was Andy Stapp. Maybe I could find him and talk, Ron said.

I found Andy the next day. At first he regarded my eagerness to talk with some suspicion, but he gave me a copy of *Vietnam, Vietnam,* by Felix Greene, and we made arrangements to meet again. Here is how Andy describes that first meeting in his book *Up Against the Brass* (New York: Simon and Schuster, 1970): "One day a tall, dark-haired eighteen-year-old came to the

Barracks looking for me. He bumped into (Paul) Gaedtke and asked where I was.

" 'What do you want him for?' Gaedtke asked suspiciously.

'I heard about his stand against the war. I want to help.'

His name was Richard Perrin and he had volunteered for the Army...."

So I took Greene's book back to the barracks and read it. The book was much more critical of the U.S. war effort than the others I had read, but by then I was receptive to its message.

By early July, I was recommending the book to my parents. That letter, which recounted some of the research I had been doing on Vietnam, provoked their concern about the "drastic change" in my correspondence with them. Here are some excerpts from my response, dated July 15, 1967:

> Yes, I guess there was a drastic change in my letters. You are right, I never did write anything to make you think I opposed the war. However, you do know that I doubted it right along. I have seen your reactions to Ron's opinions in the past. You have said many times you do not agree with them even though you do little or no research into the reasons for his opinions. It is for that reason I have not written you or talked with you about the war bothering me. If you don't believe me, go look at the letters I was writing to Ron at the same time I wrote those letters to you.
>
> I don't care if you tell Ron about that letter I wrote you in April [the one in which I said that Ron might be off his rocker], because I already have. If you're interested, I'll tell you why I wrote that letter.
>
> The stand I'm taking against the war is completely my own judgment. You can't tell me I don't hear the other side of the story. Remember I am in the Army and this is talked about constantly by fellow GIs, NCOs and officers.
>
> You can tell me that some of the atrocities are not true, but I am in contact with Vietnam veterans every day. I have heard of them tell of these horrible things. Some make me sick by laughing and joking about it, while others who are good men tell how GIs get direct orders from NCOs and officers to do these things and have no choice. Some of these men who are sick and tired of this criminal war have signed witness statements and some have even admitted committing these crimes...
>
> You think I should go to Vietnam, if my orders state so, and watch these things happening and support them just so

I can come home a good boy with the respect of the people in town. If you can present an argument by you or someone else that holds water, I will listen and consider it just as I have antiwar people's ideas.

I talked with a Catholic priest from Oklahoma City two weeks ago who is proud to see some GIs stand up to what is right. I also have written statements by other clergy and prominent men who support antiwar GIs.

I am sorry everyone at home is miserable, but there are millions in Vietnam who are just a little more miserable than you and I [don't] want to make them any more miserable than they are now.

I am sorry you can't understand the way I feel but I am sure that later you will see I am right....

When I met Andy Stapp the next time, he was with some other guys and we talked for hours. He scared me a bit. His politics were far more radical than anything I'd ever heard. He called himself a communist and for me that was radical.

Physically, there was nothing unusual about Andy— medium height, medium build. He made a point of being as sloppy looking as he could be and still get away with it as a soldier. Like other activists I have met since, he lived and breathed politics. There was nothing else in life. You couldn't talk about baseball or girls or cars or anything else, just politics. He was affiliated with a leftist group in New York called Youth Against War and Fascism. A couple of them, Ernie and Maryann Weissman came to help us out. I was grateful for the help, but found that about the only thing we had in common was our opposition to the war. Anyway, I wasn't with Andy long enough to get close to him. It all happened so fast at Fort Sill.

Andy had been confronting the military at least since the day he burned his draft card in October, 1965. Penn State kicked him out of school for that. The following May he joined the Army. Before long he was court-martialed and sentenced to forty-five days at hard labor for refusing to turn over so-called subversive literature. Not long after I was with him at Fort Sill he founded the American Servicemen's Union, which must have been the first attempt to unionize the U.S. military. The Army finally discharged him as "undesirable" in April 1969.

47

G . I . Resister

In *Up Against the Brass* Andy calls me one of his group's "strongest activist allies." However that may be, it wasn't long after we got together that I issued a statement that got picked up on newswires nationwide. Apart from some elements of my story I have told in earlier chapters, I said that I hoped "the people of the United States will wake up to the fact that they are being led through a period that will one day be called the darkest in our history. The world's people will condemn the United States, just as they condemned Hitler. I hope we antiwar GIs can count on support for our efforts." It seems I had suddenly landed in the fight with both feet.

A few days after I issued that statement, I went with two other guys (I have forgotten some names; it was a long time ago) to visit Ernie and Maryann in the Lawton motel room where they were organizing student support at the University of Oklahoma for the GI antiwar struggle. Ernie had to go back to New York shortly after that visit. Maryann remained with another antiwar activist, Key Martin. Their presence was soon publicized and an enraged mob besieged the motel. The police came and took them away. Immediately after their release from jail fourteen hours later, they set up shop in nearby Norman and continued their antiwar activities.

Before they were arrested, the Lawton police chief told the *Oklahoma City Times* that the motel was under "constant surveillance." Apparently that was true, because when we left there one night another guy and I soon realized that we were being followed by two men in an unmarked car. When we turned into a service station to fill up, the unmarked car pulled up behind us. The two men jumped out, rushed to either side of our car, yanked the doors open, pulled us out and dragged us back to their car. They shoved us against their car, put our hands on the roof, kicked our feet apart and frisked us. The guy who manhandled me gave me a good shot to the crotch when he searched the inside of my legs. It all happened so fast that I was stunned and could hardly believe it when he cuffed me and shoved me into the back seat. I hit the seat on my cuffed hands behind my back, which was not pleasant.

The two men didn't identify themselves or say anything about charges or rights; they just drove us off, to where we didn't know. On the way, we sang a few bars of "We Shall Overcome." They were not amused. We ended up at a building in downtown Lawton. They separated us and I was taken to a cell.

You know, I wish I could remember who it was that I was arrested with that night, but I just don't.

Apart from the toilet in the back corner, the cell was empty. I don't remember being scared, although I probably should have been. After a while, I stretched out on the concrete floor and went to sleep. By then a tough, hard resolve had taken over in me. I hadn't done anything wrong. Who the hell were those chumps to treat me like that?

Later that night two military policemen came to pick me up and drive me back to my unit. Our sergeant met me at the barracks. Nothing was said of charges, nor was there any explanation of the arrest. He just told me to get to my bunk. Nothing was said for the next couple of days. I simply went about my normal routine.

Finally, I was called in to see the company commander. He said I was going to be charged because I hadn't signed out on the pass register. There was nothing unusual about that. We all carried a pass. Officially, we were supposed to sign the register before we left the base, but most of us usually didn't do it. It was apparent the Army had been trying to find something they could pin on me after my arrest and the pass register was the only thing they could come up with. The company commander, a captain, whose name I can't recall, said I was being put on restriction. Other than when at school, I was to go no further than a specified distance from my barracks.

As the captain dismissed me, he told the sergeant that he wanted to see my squad leader. "Sir, Private Perrin is the squad leader," the sergeant said. Not anymore.

Several days passed without any further word. What punishment was the Army going to exact for my heinous crime? Finally I asked to see the captain. He said he would let me know the next day. Then we had a long discussion about the faults and merits of U.S. policy in Vietnam. Although I can't remember much about him—except that he had a friendly face, not the hard-bitten soldier type—I came to like the guy. I went away feeling he had a genuine concern for my well-being.

The next day, true to his word, the captain called me in and told me I was being charged with a pass violation and was subject to an Article 15 (nonjudicial company punishment). That was not severe, maybe I would have to pull a few hours extra duty for a couple weeks, probably in the kitchen, and it didn't stay on your record.

My response was ready and I delivered it without hesitation: "I want a court-martial, sir." The captain's mouth fell open. He asked again if I would sign the papers admitting my guilt. I refused.

Several days later the captain called me in again. He said the court-martial date was set and there were additional charges of breaking restriction. No explanation was offered. I couldn't figure out how I broke restriction.

When the written charges were finally delivered, I found out. Across the parking lot from my barracks there was a baseball diamond and bleachers. I had paced it off and estimated that it was about the limit of my restriction. Twice I'd gone over there to sit in the bleachers and watch a game. Those were the two charges for breaking restriction. They must have measured it with a tape.

As the day of the court-martial approached, I didn't feel isolated. I was maintaining contact with Stapp's Youth Against War and Fascism people by phone, so they knew what was going on. And some of the antiwar soldiers came by the barracks to visit me.

My hope was that by demanding a court-martial I would bring public attention to the presence of antiwar soldiers in the military. The only way to change U.S. policy in Vietnam, it seemed to me, was to build a public consensus against that policy. With that in mind, I wrote a letter to the *New York Times* saying that I was an antiwar GI.

Also, I thought that going public with my situation would give me a measure of self-defense. Some of the sergeants and officers at the school were getting aggressive. They would call me aside and berate me. I enjoyed those arguments and was pleased that other soldiers heard.

One day a major came to see me and we had quite a set-to. I tried to reason with him, but he was in a blind rage. His only argument was a rote patriotic line about how we lived in the greatest country in the world, we were the greatest people in the world and people in other countries had better toe the line. I asked him if he was saying that people born in France, Canada or, for that matter, Vietnam were inferior to us simply because they were born somewhere else. He said that was what he believed.

I called Ron and asked him if he would come to Oklahoma for the court-martial. He came. His support was important. I was elated when I saw him walking toward my barracks. He was with the lawyer YAWF had obtained to defend me. But the Army wouldn't let Ron and me get together to talk and that was frustrating.

The lawyer was from the Emergency Civil Liberties Union. His name was Rudolf Schwere. I learned that he had been with the Abraham Lincoln Brigade during the Spanish Civil War, one of the American groups that fought with the Republicans against Franco. We had little time to talk about Spain, but enough for me to know that I had a lot to learn.

All the soldiers on the base were called to formation outside their barracks on the morning of the court-martial. They were informed of the charges against me and two other soldiers who were being court-martialed that same day elsewhere on the base. It was good of the Army to spread the news. Everyone was told to stay away from the proceedings.

The base was declared off-limits to civilians. It was usually open to anyone. Several people from around the United States had traveled to Oklahoma to attend the courts-martial. Key Martin and Maryann Weissman attempted to come onto the base anyway and were arrested. Later they were tried, convicted and sentenced to jail terms. Probably because he was family, Ron was allowed to attend the trial.

As I walked to the court-martial building, I was astounded to see scores of military police around. And, to my amazement, helicopters were circling overhead, probably watching for unauthorized Americans who thought they had a right to attend a trial. I think of that day whenever I hear someone ask in frustration, "What can one person do?"

There wasn't much of a defense for my crimes. I had not signed out on the pass register and I guess the bleachers at the ball field were outside the restriction limits. I was convicted and sentenced to thirty days at hard labor.

On the way to the stockade, I talked with the guard marching me at gunpoint. He was black. I suggested that Vietnam was not his war any more than it was mine and asked what the hell he was doing leading me around with his gun. He was plainly uncomfortable. He knew I was no criminal. According to Stapp's book *Up Against the Brass*, the guard "was so upset that he went AWOL and wasn't picked up until a month later."

I was put into a holding cage just inside the stockade gate. Prisoners gathered around, curious to see the "communist GI." They had copies of the local Lawton newspaper with the story of the court-martial. That was the only newspaper I ever saw in there. Evidently, the stockade commander thought the prisoners might dish out a little punishment of their own.

Before long, I was ushered into the commander's office. He was a short man with dark hair, probably of southern European stock, and he had the pugnacious air of a little guy with something to prove. He stepped up to me, shoved his face close to mine and screamed insults. His saliva was running off my face as he glared up at me. He stepped back a few times and feigned punches. Clearly, he was trying to provoke me into defending myself, but one touch and he could charge me with assaulting an officer. I held my ground, tried not to flinch. He was out to get me and I knew it.

They put me in a stockade barracks for only a short while and then the commander called me back to his office. He told me he had been directed to send me to a high security compound where I would be isolated from the prison population for my own protection. He said he regretted that.

Guards escorted me to another room where my head was sheared to stubble. The higher security area was apart from the main stockade compound. I climbed into the back of a truck with an armed guard and they drove me there. The cells were in the basement of a concrete building. I remember going through a steel doorway then down the stairs to the cellblock. The cells looked like gorilla cages in old zoos. Some housed several inmates.

The guards paraded me around the cellblock and it was clear that the prisoners were waiting for me, the "communist GI." They banged on the bars of their cells and shouted obscenities at me. My cell was at the further end on the south side. It was about forty-two feet square (6' x 7'). The bunk was of plate steel hinged to the wall and hung by chains at either end. The guards said that there were no mattresses or blankets left.

But this was Oklahoma in late July and I didn't need a blanket. A mattress would have helped. The plate steel was no feather bed. I slept in my boxer shorts on top of my fatigue uniform. Three walls of the cell were solid steel, the front barred. I could see slits of sky through the windows above. I couldn't see the other prisoners but I could hear them.

To use the latrine, I had to call for the turnkey, as the guards were called. They usually took their time coming and sometimes I thought my bladder would burst.

It wasn't long before the prisoners close enough to talk with me realized that I wasn't a monster and the word got around. We had discussions about the war. The prisoner on one side had a deck of cards. Though we couldn't see each other, we played cards by reaching through the bars. He taught me to play gin rummy.

Apart from the awful meals, always served cold, the only thing they gave us was cigarettes. At first I traded them for cheap paperbacks, but I soon started smoking some to alleviate the boredom. The habit stayed with me for thirty years.

One night a guy screaming for mercy woke me up. What I heard told me that another prisoner, a bigger man no doubt, was forcing him to give him a blow job while the guards watched. I could hear the guards laughing and the scene those sounds created for me was as ugly and disgusting as any I have ever encountered.

The stockade commander came around to see me several times. He was beside himself because he couldn't get his hands on me. I was glad there had been so much publicity surrounding the court-martial.

One day he stood outside of my cell and worked himself into a rage. Finally, he had the turnkey let one of the guys next to me out of his cell, not the prisoner I played cards with, but the guy on the other side. The commander grabbed the man, forced him down and kicked the crap out of him. It was a vicious beating and when it was over the commander turned to me, smiled and said, "I wish I could do that to you."

I still feel guilty because I never did anything about the beating that man took in my stead. After I got out I could have blown the whistle on that runty commander, but I never did. I just wanted to get out of that hellhole and stay out.

The next day they put another prisoner in with me. He was the biggest, meanest looking, scarred-up character I had ever seen. He looked at me and the first thing he said was, "I hate white people." I thought I was as good as dead. He told me later he was Apache, jailed for stabbing an officer.

I offered him the bunk and then set about assuring him that I was not his enemy. Thankfully, he decided he could tolerate me and we ended up having some good conversations. He told me about life on the reservation. He was an angry guy and like the black guy in basic training he sure didn't feel that the U.S. Army was his army. Anyway, he was with me only a day or so.

But his presence reminded me that the Apache warrior Geronimo had done time at Fort Sill. In the old stockade there, not in use in 1967, is a row of cells. If I remember correctly, the walls are stone, no windows to the outside, and thick wooden doors with a small window barely bigger than a peephole. That was where Geronimo was held, at least for a time. Otherwise he and his people were kept on a corner of the fort as prisoners of war. I like to believe that had I been alive in the late nineteenth century I would have been sympathetic to the cause of the Apaches. Maybe the Apache man who was thrown into the cell with me knew that somehow. In any case, that I have the Fort Sill stockade experience in common with both Geronimo and my Apache cellmate makes me feel good.

Not long after they pulled the Apache guy out of my cell, several officers, including my friend the chaplain, the one who didn't think people should act out of conscience, came to see me. They tried to convince me of the error of my ways and I enjoyed the debate. Then one day one of the officers showed up and ordered me to come with him to his office.

Just like that we walked out of the security compound, got into his car and drove to his office. We walked in and there were my mother and father waiting for us, both of them looking anguished. Apparently the Army had convinced them they should come and talk some sense into me.

It was obviously a difficult time for them. They couldn't understand what was happening. They blamed Ron and I was annoyed that they didn't give me credit for having a mind of my own.

What a sight I must have seemed to them. The guards hadn't allowed me to shower or shave and my fatigues were filthy. I stood there looking like a bum, no doubt reeking, and that seemed to upset them all the more.

I wish I could remember more of what was said in that room. It was all something of a whirl. But I do remember that my parents were more distraught than I had ever seen them and when they asked me to stop the antiwar activity and apologize to the officer, I apologized. They went back to Vermont somewhat relieved and I went back to my cell.

There was an exchange of letters between my father and Ron shortly after the Oklahoma visit. Some excerpts from them may help to clarify the deep division in my family after I was court-martialed. My father wrote first:

Dear Ronald,

I have tried several times to write to you but whatever I would say you would use against me. Anyway I told you I would write so I will try to tell you how I feel about this mess.

When I called you up and asked you not to tell Dick the things you were telling him, you kept saying that I was accusing you. All I was trying to do was ask you not to interfere with Dick's Army life. Because back in June Dick showed me a letter that you wrote to him and that letter was pure poison. I can agree with some of the things you say. A lot of things are not right. But it seems to me that if you are concerned about Sasha and the rest of your family that you stop and think of the good things in this country. With the education you have now you can help to make things better. But by trying to destroy our country?

I can't for the life of me understand why you want to be different from everybody else. I'm sure your own mother would not want you to be this way....

For a long time I looked forward to a grandson and I was proud of you going back to school. And then it had to turn out this way. Not very rewarding after the heartache caring for you when you were a child. We brought up Dick, Nancy and

David to look up to you as a good brother and then you turn around and use Dick.

I know you think I'm an old fool. But you will be surprised what you learn when you get to be my age....

You told me on the phone that you kept Dick from going AWOL. Well you must think we are pretty stupid because we read some of the books that you had Dick read and they were enough to make him want to go AWOL.

All I can say [is] why don't you ask Sandra. She can tell you what it is like in some other countries. And if you tried to do what you have done here you wouldn't be around long to tell about it....

All I can say, Ronald, the last few months you have made it rough on Betty and me and very costly. And worse yet the record Dick will have the rest of his life.

Now it is up to you the kind of life you want. Think about Sandra and Sasha. As for Betty and me we were brought up to be good American citizens and plan to stay that way.

It must be a lonely life for you. But think what it will do to the rest of your family. And if you continue like this we will have to keep Nancy and David from the same thing you did to Dick.

I pray to God that you may again be the Ronald I used to know as my loving son. I also think of my fine grandson, Sasha. When you watch the children going to school you watch the children play and you think of Sasha. I'm sure you would want him to be like the rest.

You can have a great future or you can mess up the rest of your life.

I can tell you this I have found out about your activities and I was shocked. Any system that will turn you against your family and can't tell you the truth to me is no better than ours....

Ron's response is dated 14 September. A lot had happened by then. After my parent's visit at Fort Sill, officers I hadn't seen before visited me in the stockade. It was clear they were trying to cut a deal. They said if I stopped my antiwar efforts and broke my contacts with antiwar groups, the Army would assign me to Germany for the rest of my hitch. I agreed. By then I would have done about anything to get out of that hole. For one thing, I was trying to save my own hide. Between the incidents with the stockade commander and my Apache cellmate—whose formidable presence was probably no accident—I had some doubts about my safety if I stayed there much longer.

So I was released after serving fifteen days. It seemed more like fifteen months. After our deal was closed and I was released, the officers told me that the charges, the severe sentence and everything else was their attempt to stop my fight against the war.

Ron's letter was written after I had relocated to Germany. A lot was happening then that no one else knew about.

Dear Dad,

I am glad that you were finally able to write me. There have been many times when I have been down and started to write to you but after Dick told me that you had been trying to explain my activities over the past two years in terms of my grandparents mental illness I gave up ever trying to get you to understand what I believe and what I am doing. I won't try anymore except to tell you despite what you have probably heard I am not a communist, that I haven't undergone some huge change since you last saw me, and I am not different from everyone else. You know that because you listen to the radio and watch the news. There are thousands of good Americans who feel as I do about the Negro and about the war.

You said that I lied to you on the phone that night. I said then that I had never approached Dick and talked against the war but that I had answered him when he asked me how I felt. After I wrote him the letter which he showed you he wrote back and said he was glad to have my opinion but he thought this was something he was going to have to figure out for himself. I agreed with him and that was it. Since then I have only answered when he asked. (Incidentally, it cost me a lot to go to Oklahoma too. I had to borrow the money but Dick asked me to go and so I went.)

Don't misunderstand me. I am not denying that I am to some degree responsible for Dick's attitude now. But you want to make me totally responsible and when you do that you make Dick out to be some sort of dumb puppy instead of a man, old enough to go off and die for his country. If he didn't believe in what he was doing I don't think he would have been able to go through what he went through in Oklahoma. He could have taken company punishment instead of the court-martial but he made the decision—I didn't even know of it until he had decided.

Nor am I responsible for his hatred of racial prejudice, that is something we both learned from you a long time ago. You have always said it was bad. I mention this now because the last letter I got from him he was pretty upset about the prejudice in his company in Germany. Apparently one of his buddies got beat up by whites for speaking favorably about Negroes. I wrote Dick and said he would probably meet some better guys soon. I didn't go into a long speech against race hatred or anything else, as I would have done if I were, as you insist, using Dick. No wonder you think I am crazy, if you think I am using my brother then I would have to be crazy.

I asked you several times on the phone to talk with Dick, not to him by ordering him around but with him. You promised that you would but instead you ordered him to straighten out and told him you would have others speak to him about the war. He didn't give a damn if you knew less than he did, it was you he wanted to talk with. But then he wrote to [the Rev.] Henderson and he tells me that Henderson said he supported him. If this is true then I am not the only one who thinks this way and I am not solely responsible for Dick's actions. But if you insist that I am and nothing I have said or can say will change your mind.

He wants to speak with you about these things. I know he does, but he can't until you start listening. He says he spoke with you and Betty the night before he came out here and you said later you didn't remember. He wrote a confidential letter to Betty when you were out here and she showed it to you. Do you wonder why he came to talk to me? These things are important to him and you have to listen. If you won't then you are also responsible when he turns to someone else.

I'm not saying these things to hurt you, there has been enough hurt all around. But because you have two other children and whether you forbid them to talk to me or not, they are going to talk with someone if you don't start treating your kids like thinking human beings. As far as Betty's note about never interfering in Sasha's life all I can say is that if Sasha comes to you when he is 18 because he couldn't talk to me then I hope you will "interfere."

I know you both love us all very much but there has to be more than love, there has to be respect.

Soon after I was released from the stockade I received orders for Germany with a stopover of several days at Fort Dix, New Jersey. Mom and Dad came down to visit me there. That morning, before they arrived, I was sent out on a detail picking up litter from road ditches around the base. I wasn't in my barracks and my folks were told that I was AWOL. MPs were sent out looking for me, but I was nowhere to be found. At five that afternoon our detail returned to the unit in the same truck we'd left in that morning. I was spotted and told to report to the company headquarters.

When my story was confirmed, the company commander, out of embarrassment I suppose, agreed, at my parents insistence, to give me a week's leave so I could visit before I went overseas. We drove up to Vermont that evening. Oddly enough, I remember almost nothing of that visit—an indication perhaps, of how wide the gap had grown between me and the life I had been raised to live. In any case, that was the last time I would see Vermont in ten years.

After returning to Fort Dix from that unscheduled leave, I had to wait for new travel orders to Germany. Late one night we were awakened by a commotion outside the barracks. We rushed out and saw spotlights trained on a water tower in the middle of a nearby field. There was a man on the tower yelling down at the MPs. We edged closer and could hear him threatening to jump if the Army didn't promise to send him home. I don't know what the MPs said to him, but he came down after a while.

That is one of the last images of my Army tour in the States: a man threatening to leap off a tower in the middle of the night. Little did I know that I was about to take a leap myself and that it would be another decade before I ever set foot on U.S. soil again.

GERMANY 1967

A chartered Caribbean Airlines flight got me to Frankfurt. After landing, we had to wait around until our ground transportation was ready. Fresh from the States, we were curious about Army life in Germany. We asked some of the soldiers waiting to fly out about it. One of the first comments I heard was that we could forget about German girls because "they go for the niggers."

Finally, we climbed onto a bus and headed down the autobahn to Kitzingen, which is in south-central Germany near the city of Würzburg. The base was just outside that picturesque town. I was told that it was formerly a Nazi Luftwaffe base that the U.S. Army had converted to armor.

When I reported for duty, it was obvious that the commanding officer was not aware of my political history. He looked at my records and remarked that thirty days hard labor was pretty severe punishment for the minor charges I had faced. Then he told me he had a surplus of track vehicle mechanics and that after a soldier was trained in his selected field the Army was under no obligation to use him there. I thought of the recruiter making his pitch in Rutland. I told the commander that I had made some serious decisions based upon that training and I really wanted to work as a mechanic. He decided that, in view of how well I had done in both training schools, he would use me as a mechanic.

Later I attended an orientation session for new arrivals. They showed us slides of East German and Czech license plates and told us to report any that we saw. They also warned us about crossing the East German border inadvertently. From what I'd heard about the Iron Curtain, I wondered how anyone could get across that border inadvertently.

Evenings, we liked to sit around the enlisted men's club and drink beer out of those nifty bottles with the porcelain and wire flip tops. I began hearing those macho military stories again. Some of the soldiers had been in Vietnam. Others who had been in Germany for a while told us how much they enjoyed plowing their tanks through German farm fields, ripping up soil and damaging crops. And I heard countless stories about how much some of those GIs enjoyed abusing German women. Some of them seemed to think the women were fair game for just about anything simply because they were German and not American.

Can it be, I wonder now, that it was as bad as it sounded? Or was it a lot of brainless chest beating? But that attitude was prevalent at the Kitzingen base. The German people were "inferior"—not only the civilians, but the German military as well. Not all the GIs were like that, of course, but enough of them so that sometimes the very air seemed fouled and it was hard not to breathe it in.

Then one Saturday night in a club a black guy walked in with a German woman. Someone yelled a racial insult and the fight was on—punching and wrestling, tables and chairs flying, bottles breaking. I got the hell out of there. On those Saturday nights, with half the GIs drunk and the other half stoned, some both, I wondered what would have happened if the Red Army had attacked.

For several weeks I tried to mind my own business, keep my mouth shut, stick to the deal I'd made, but my disgust with the Army was growing. I'd get up in the morning and put on my fatigue uniform and feel ashamed of wearing it. That was a far cry from my first weeks in the service. I was disgusted with it all, with basic training, with Vietnam, with what was going on in Germany. It became clear that I wanted to spend my time in the struggle to end the war in Vietnam; I didn't want to spend it fooling around with tanks in West Germany and participating in all that bigoted crap any longer.

Besides, I began to feel that I was being watched. I started placing hairs in the books I kept in my locker. Sure enough, I'd come back after duty hours and find the hairs I strategically placed were missing. That was not part of the deal I'd made with the Army. I had, to that point, kept up my end.

I knew that if I started talking about the war again they would find a way to isolate me and I vowed that I wouldn't let them cage me up again. I just wanted it all to stop and I knew that my conscience would not rest unless I made a concerted effort, as individual and insignificant as it might be, to get American soldiers out of Vietnam. The Army was not going to allow that, so I started making plans to leave.

By this time I was not the same young man I'd been just a few months earlier. I was hardened and not afraid. I was ready to take on some powerful forces. I disregarded my own welfare and with some shame now, I admit I disregarded the welfare of my family, too.

I needed money so I waited for payday at the end of the month. Conveniently, I was given a twelve-hour pass on Saturday of the Labor Day weekend. I communicated absolutely nothing of my plans to anyone. I recall giving some of my military clothing to another guy. He must have wondered about me.

On Saturday, I went to the Kitzingen railroad station and boarded a train for Heidelberg, which was only about fifty miles to the southwest. Concerned that anything larger might tip off my intentions, I carried only a small bag and was constantly alert for anyone that might be watching me. So began my life on the lam and I got good at it.

Before leaving, I had decided to head for France rather than Sweden. Most of us knew that neutral Sweden was accepting U.S. deserters. France seemed riskier, but relations between Paris and Washington were not the best so I thought it worth the risk. At France's request, U.S. troops were no longer stationed on French soil, as they had been since the end of World War II. Not only that, but I had a French family background on my Dad's side. Even in my imagination Paris felt more comfortable to me, so that was my destination.

Outside the Heidelberg station, I asked a cab driver his fare to a village called Heiligkreuzsteinach. My cousin Tim McCarthy, who had the year earlier been in Poway when I was there, was living in Heiligkreuzsteinach and I was hoping I could convince him to drive me to France. The taxi fare was reasonable so I hopped in. We rumbled off over the cobblestones, crossed the Neckar River and were soon winding up into the mountains. Heiligkreuzsteinach huddled in a narrow valley. The driver dropped me at an inn perched on a ridge above the village. Ron had given me Tim's phone number. I called it but there was no answer. I didn't like staying overnight in Germany. My pass was good from Saturday noon to midnight. After midnight I would be AWOL. But, seeing no alternative, I registered at the hotel and ate a hearty German meal in the dining room. The hotel people were friendly, but I was wary about too much exposure so I retired early.

Up in my room, I considered burning my military ID card in the sink, but then thought better of it. That was a lucky second thought because the ID card came in handy later on.

I had a good night's sleep, that I still remember. I always slept well in those days, even on the floor of an Oklahoma jail cell the night I was arrested. Maybe it's part of being young.

In the morning, I went downstairs, had coffee and pastry, and then tried Tim's number again. This time he answered. I told him where I was and he said he would be right over to pick me up. A short time later he drove up in a little Fiat sedan. Man, was I relieved to see a familiar face.

It turned out that Tim lived on the hill across the valley. On that sunny Sunday morning, we could see his house from my hotel. As we drove back through the valley, I told him what I was up to. He asked me if I had considered the consequences of going AWOL. We talked it over briefly, but when we got to his house he asked me to be quiet about it in front of his wife's sister, Arlette, who was visiting from France.

The house had three rooms and a spacious hallway upstairs. Sliding glass doors in the living/dining room opened onto a patio and a broad view of the valley. Tim said the owner worked as a nurse in Alberta, Canada. We all talked for a while. Tim's wife Jeannine was as pert and pretty as ever. Arlette was plainer, plumper, but she seemed to accept me as part of the family. She had worked for the U.S. Army and knew some English. Finally, Arlette and Jeannine went out to sit in the sun on the patio. Tim cracked one of the beers he had delivered to his door every week, like they used to deliver milk in the States, and we sat at the small kitchen table and talked about my plans.

As luck would have it, they were getting ready to drive Arlette back to her home in Verdun, site of the horrendous battle in eastern France in World War I. Tim had been stationed there in the late 1950s, which was how he met Jeannine. He seemed reluctant about taking me to France, but I told him I was going to do it whether he helped me or not.

So the four of us piled into the Fiat, along with Tim's overweight beagle, Clea, and headed south. I was in the back seat with Arlette and the dog. After working our way down out of the mountains toward Heidelberg, we came to an east-west intersection. Tim stopped the car, turned to me and said, "East or West?" I said, "West. Let's go to France." By then Arlette must have known something was going on.

Rather than heading directly west, we traveled south along the Rhine to an obscure border crossing Tim knew about not far below Strasbourg. He thought we would have a better chance there. I don't recall being too nervous when I left my unit in Kitzingen, but I was sure nervous as we approached that border crossing. We talked about putting me in the trunk, but decided that if the border guards decided to check there I would be finished. There would be no way to talk our way out of it. So we made a last-minute plan that if problems developed I would bolt from the car and run as far as I could into French territory. That was probably a good way to get shot. Later I developed better ways to cross borders.

Because Jeannine worked for the Army, the Fiat had U.S. forces license plates and I'm sure that helped. The Germans waved us through. As we crossed the narrow bridge into France, I had my hand on the door handle. I was already thankful I hadn't burned my military ID card. Apart from that, all I had to show was a California driver's license and that wouldn't get me far.

Tim rolled down his window as the guard approached. The guard leaned down and looked us over then asked if Tim had rabies vaccination papers for the dog. Tim dug into his travel documents. It took him so long to find the vaccination certificate that the guard got impatient. But that must have distracted him because he never asked the rest of us for any documentation. Off we drove into France, no questions asked. I've often thought that the gods must have been riding with us that day.

We drove up into the Vosges Mountains to the village of Saint-Amé, where my grandfather is buried. His gravestone is carved from gleaming red granite, by far the most imposing in the cemetery—a sign, I guess, that his granite business was the village's biggest employer. Tim said he and Jeannine had come there on their honeymoon in 1958 because they couldn't afford to go anywhere else. He said our grandfather treated them well. Rich as Marius Perrin was, he lived in a cramped apartment up over a pharmacy in a building he owned.

From Saint-Amé, we drove out of the mountains, through the bustling city of Nancy and on to Verdun. Jeannine's mother, Rachel, greeted us warmly. We stayed that night in her three-room apartment on the third floor of an ancient stone building. There was a chamber pot in the bedroom.

The next morning we had café au lait in big white bowls, and ate hunks of buttered bread fresh from the bakery a few doors down the street. Then Tim and I set off for Paris, little knowing what a long day that would be. It was about a four-hour drive, mostly through rolling farmland, village after village. We stopped for a rest at Châlons-sur-Marne, a larger town about halfway between Verdun and Paris. Tim told me about a similar trip he'd made in 1959. He was on his way back to the States to be discharged from the Army. A sergeant he worked with had offered to drive him to Paris in the big white Oldsmobile he had just imported from the States. Another soldier rode along. They stopped in Châlons and downed a few shots of cognac. As they headed on into Paris, Tim and the other soldier told the sergeant he was driving too fast. The road was narrow and had a high crown. Big American cars did not corner well on it. Then on a curve at the top of a hill the car skidded, slammed into a guardrail and rolled three times before landing on its wheels, horn blaring. Tim and the other soldier were not badly hurt but the sergeant had been thrown out and his neck was broken. An Army ambulance finally got them back to the military hospital in Verdun. It was Sunday and the Army staff hustled Tim out of there fast because he had travel orders. He found Jeannine and they took the evening train to Paris. He was twenty years old and glad to be alive.

That was pretty much the way I felt when we arrived in Paris that noon. I needed help and we didn't have any contacts, so we looked up addresses in a phone book and started making the rounds of leftist political parties and publications, magazines such as *Le Nouvel Observateur*. Everyone was suspicious. I had a folder with newspaper clippings from my court-martial in Oklahoma, which we hoped would convince people that I was a genuine resister, but that didn't seem to help much. One of our briefest and rudest encounters was in the office of the Communist newspaper *L'humanité*, which struck me as odd. We even tried to contact the philosopher Jean-Paul Sartre, because Tim knew he was involved in antiwar activities, but he was not in the phone book, of course, and no one admitted having his number. (I later spoke at an antiwar rally with Sartre and I used to see him at various cafes, always with some young woman.)

Finally, late in the afternoon, when we were both dragging our asses a bit, some students at the Sorbonne told us about the Quakers. We drove around until we found the address. A bearded, gray-haired man with a gentle air greeted us in his small, spartan office lined with books. He was a Brit named Tony Clay and he knew instantly what we wanted and said he could put me in touch with people who could help me.

Tim was relieved because he could head back to Verdun. Jeannine had to be at work the next day. He thanked Tony profusely. Tony said that was fine if it made him feel any better about leaving his friend on his own in Paris. Tim said I knew how to get hold of him and he could be there in a few hours if I needed him.

Before he left, Tim taught me a few French phrases that would help me to survive. I learned how to ask for a camembert sandwich, a salami sandwich and a quarter liter of red table wine. That's pretty much what I ate and drank during my first days in Paris.

At that hour, Tony couldn't get in touch with anyone, so he found me a room in a hotel just around the corner. He knew the owners and they allowed me to stay there without the proper documentation. There I was, alone on the first night of what turned out to be my tumultuous stay in Paris.

PARIS 1967

The next morning I went down to the lobby, had a croissant and coffee and waited to hear from Tony. The wait seemed endless, but finally Tony called and said a man would be coming to see me. He said the man's name was Max Cook.

Max turned out to be one of the most incredible people I've ever met. He showed up late for our appointment, which I later learned, was typical. But it was hard to get mad at him even when he was late. He would make you smile. And that first morning in Paris he was about all I had.

So there he was, short, heavyset, a perpetual five o'clock shadow, unruly brown hair, speaking fluent English with a German accent, a bundle of energy, a dynamo. He always seemed to be in a hurry, always running a bit late with a few too many irons in the fire. He walked fast, drove fast, tore in and out of traffic on those narrow Parisian streets until your hair stood on end. His mind worked faster than he drove, his mouth faster still.

Max did not embrace me at first, not by a long shot. He was there that day to grill me, to find if I was for real or if I was an agent. But I didn't realize that at the time. I showed him my newspaper clippings from Fort Sill and that made him even more suspicious. My story was too good to be true. He later told me he was pretty much convinced I was an agent. I came to know his technique well. He was like that detective Peter Falk played on television, Colombo, always pretending that he was a little bit behind what was happening. But Max was highly intelligent, a geophysicist from Vienna who wanted badly to be just an ordinary guy.

Years later I read about Max in James Reston Jr's book *The Amnesty of John David Herndon* (New York: McGraw-Hill, 1973). Herndon was a deserter who traveled much the same route I did into Paris, though later, probably after I left Paris. He ended up at the Quaker Center where he met Tony Clay. Tony put him in touch with Max and Max grilled him. As Reston puts it: "Max's interrogation of John was tough and thorough. John described it as tougher than anything the CIA could stage. And John, who would claim that he had conducted similar interrogations of *arrivés* later, accepted completely the need for it: to ferret out stool pigeons for the Army's CID (Criminal Investigation Division) or the CIA. John's interrogation began:

Max: 'What's your father's name?'

John: 'What's it to you...?'

Max (in Viennese English): 'Shut the fuck up and tell your father's name....'

Max was the one, according to John, who would say to Tony, " 'I'll chance him,' or 'I don't want to mess with him.'

'If he'd chance you, he'd give you some money, find you some work, and a place to stay. If you screwed up, that was it.' "

That was the way it happened with me, although I don't remember Max being that tough when he grilled me at the hotel that first morning. Anyway, I stayed at the hotel another night and the next day Max came to pick me up. He drove me to the avenue de la République on the Right Bank, where he had arranged a place for me to stay. He gave me a hundred francs, about twenty dollars at the time. I didn't see much of him for the next few weeks and that was frustrating. But I did come to like the man a lot after he finally came around and began spending time with me.

No matter where we went in Paris, no matter down what street, Max had a story to tell about it. Usually it was a historical or political story: Vladimir Lenin lived on this street. This is where the Communards did battle in 1871. You could spend an hour with Max and learn more about history and geography than you could in any couple of months at school.

My roommate on the avenue de la République was a Vietnamese mathematics student named Tian. He had a two bedroom flat with plenty of room for both of us. There was a huge blackboard in the living room covered with mathematical equations that he sometimes talked himself through for hours at a time. There was also a grand piano in that room on which Tian played classical music. The guy was as cultured as he was smart. But, like Max, he drove like a maniac. He had this little Deux Chevaux, that gray bug of a car with canvas seats like springy lawn chairs and the shifting lever poking out of the dashboard. It was scary driving around Paris with him on those narrow streets. He'd come to an intersection and not even slow down. I'd sit there bouncing on that canvas seat and think, "Oh shit! He's going to kill us."

As it turned out, I didn't spend much time with Tian. He was seldom home. Most of the time he was off with the French woman he was dating. So, even though I stayed in his flat for several months, I never got to know him very well. I do remember that one of his parents supported the SouthVietnamese government in the war and Tian was sympathetic to the North. So at least some of his family were probably bourgeois Catholics and Tian was the renegade son who favored Ho Chi Minh.

Those first weeks in Paris were lonely. I consoled myself by wandering around the city. One day I went to the Louvre and checked out the Mona Lisa. There I met an English girl on holiday. We spent the rest of the day walking about together. It was good to find someone I could talk with.

Beyond that I was submerged in the daily routine. There was a French fry stand just around the corner from Tian's place. For someone with little money it was a lifesaver. They would wrap up my batch of fries in a newspaper, then I'd buy a half-dozen oranges and a liter of wine and that was my meal. At the wine shop downstairs, I could buy a liter of red table wine for not much more than the cost of a small bottle of Coke in the States.

Finally Max called again and told me to meet him at the famous Deux Magots café on the Left Bank. He was late as usual. I sat at a sidewalk table and read the *International Herald Tribune*. Suddenly a fist smashed down through the paper, tearing it out of my hands. An enraged Frenchman screamed at me in English: "You Americans, they should drop a nuclear bomb on you!" He was a little upset with American foreign policy, I guess, and he startled the hell out of me. Oddly enough, expressions of anti-American sentiments, whether verbal or in graffiti, really upset me. You'd think they would have given me comfort.

Finally Max showed up and we had a long conversation. We also made arrangements to go for dinner a few nights later and he introduced me to his wife, Simone, and their dog Gertrude. I think I may have been the only deserter Max took home to meet his wife. At least I don't remember seeing any of the other guys there. But we were all Max's "babies." That's what he called us. And we each had a number. I was baby number six.

Anyway, we had a wonderful dinner that night and Simone and I hit it off really well. She was a fairly plain looking woman, but there was something about her that told me she had been attractive when she was younger. Her father had been with the *maquis* during the second World War. She used to tell me stories about how her father and the others resisted the German occupation, even if only by picking off a German soldier who had strayed too far from the pack.

Simone helped me a lot. She fed me, introduced me to her friends, and was someone to talk to. She ran a little bookshop and art gallery on l'île Saint Louis, just across the footbridge behind the cathedral of Notre Dame. It was centrally located, so when I was wandering around the city in those first months I'd stop in there. "Bonjour, André," she'd say, always with a big smile, as I came in the door. André was the name I used during my first several months in France. Because I didn't have any papers to live there legally, I was living underground as André Francis, the name Max gave me. (Names were one way Max kept track of his babies. "André" began with an "A" and marked his first run through the alphabet. "Francis" began with the sixth letter of the alphabet and meant that I was his sixth baby. Years later, after I had settled into Canada, I was amused when a black guy from the States came to play in the Canadian Football League. His name was Andre Francis.

The only time Simone got impatient with me was when I pissed in her bidet. I had never seen a bidet before and I presumed it was a urinal. When Simone confronted me, I was a bit stunned at how she could so unabashedly say that a bidet was used for washing a woman's private parts. I wasn't used to hearing people speak so openly about such personal matters. It was all part of a small-town Vermonter's education in a foreign land.

That education continued. Later that fall, Max and Simone took me to Villejuif to celebrate the fiftieth anniversary of the Bolshevik Revolution. We went to see the play "Ten Days that Shook the World," based on the book by American journalist John Reed, who was in Russia during the 1917 Revolution.

In the town square of Villejuif stood a statue. It was not a statue of Rousseau, nor Jeanne d'Arc, nor Napoleon. No. It was a statue of Yuri Gagarin, the Russian space pilot, who in 1961 had become the first human to orbit the earth.

On sale at the Vietnamese pavilion at the Villejuif fair were sandals made from the tires of downed American warplanes and rings fashioned from similar wreckage, with the date of the kill engraved on the inside of each ring. A mannequin dressed in a U.S. pilot's uniform was on display. In 1967, it seemed you could find the madness of the Vietnam War just about anywhere.

So the weeks wore on in that fall of 1967. Max seemed to trust me more and more. He found me a job with an architectural firm run by a couple of Greek exiles. A right-wing military junta was in power in Athens and these guys were socialists. They hired me out of sympathy, not for any skills they could have used. I was supposed to build models from their blueprints. Using Popsicle sticks, tongue depressors and toothpicks, I struggled to construct little buildings. But I didn't have a clue how to read blueprints, so how was I supposed to look at them and visualize an apartment building? They were patient with me, but I soon told Max that I couldn't do the job and didn't feel right about accepting a salary from them (always in cash because I didn't have work papers).

Finally we learned that the French government, after some significant lobbying by antiwar activists, was going to give legal residency to American deserters. Max lined me up with a lawyer and we went off to apply for a carte de séjour at police headquarters. I have forgotten the lawyer's name, but he was an interesting guy. He had represented French journalist Régis Debray in Bolivia after he was arrested for spending time with Che Guevara's guerrillas during their hapless struggle to foment a revolution.

Across the desk from us at police headquarters sat a pompous little imitator of Charles de Gaulle. Looking stern, he sat there erectly in his starchy uniform festooned with medals, my file on the desk in front of him. His round police cap was perched on a corner of the desk. He opened my file and raised his eyebrows. *"Mais vous êtes français,"* he said. Sometimes it pays to have a French name. I think the lawyer was surprised how easily I got my residency papers.

That allowed me to get work papers as well and Max found me another job, this time as a maintenance man in an envelope factory. I worked for the head mechanic and his apprentice, Christian. I don't remember the mechanic's name, but they were both good guys. And I do remember being impressed with the way they worked together and related to the other employees.

Arriving in the morning, everyone shook hands and exchanged a friendly *"Bonjour, comment ça va."* Everybody, that is, except the owner, the *patron*. I learned fast that class distinctions are much sharper in France than they are in the United States. The head mechanic gave me hell for addressing the *patron* with the familiar *tu* rather than the formal *vous*. The owner had given me the job out of concern, but after that I addressed him the same way the other workers did.

The head mechanic was an older guy, a little stooped, about ready to retire. No doubt he had seen a lot. One day he again gave me hell because I shook hands with a German who came around to check out some of the machinery. He lectured me on what the Nazis had done in Paris and told me bluntly that it was inappropriate to shake hands with a German. That was his generation speaking. Most of the younger people I met didn't feel that way.

Part of my job was to wander around the factory oiling and greasing machinery. That was great fun because a lot of teenage girls worked there and we flirted every chance we got. My French was still weak, so most of the flirting, in fact most all conversation, was done in pantomime. They were working there waiting to get married and become housewives. That's the way it worked at that time for French girls who didn't go on to higher education.

The men loved to play practical jokes on me. My poor French made me an easy mark and we had some good laughs all around. I ran a lot of errands, usually with a written message, but if it was simple enough I memorized it. The men knew there was one girl in particular I found attractive. One day Christian pointed to her and gave me a message to repeat to her. I walked up to her and said in French (with no idea what I was saying, of course), "I have a big cock." Everyone on the factory floor broke up. What a hoot! Christian was laughing so hard he was rolling on the floor. I was laughing, too, once I figured out what was going on. Somehow being the butt of their good-natured pranks showed that they liked and accepted me.

We played a lot of language games, Christian and I. He was a small, bebopping sort of guy, light on his feet. He always wanted me to teach him off-colored English words and he did the same for me in French. Swear words made up much of my early French vocabulary. Christian knew that in our working class neighborhood the chances of running into a woman who spoke English were slim. So, armed with his new vocabulary, he would bop up to a woman on the subway and say, "Hey, baby. Want to fuck?" and that would send him into gales of laughter. He kept telling me about his sister, but he never introduced me.

There was a café on the corner by the factory where most of the men went to eat lunch. I don't know where the women went. The men liked to stand at the bar and eat. They'd have an aperitif, then a glass of wine and an omelette or something. I would sit on a bench in a little booth and study French. The man and woman who ran the café would help me with the French lessons while they served me my food.

I have often heard Americans and Canadians say they don't like going to France because the people are so unfriendly. But I seldom experienced that. Most of the French people I met were helpful. Some of them regarded draft evaders and deserters as heroes. Often, I was invited to their homes to eat. I didn't know those people; they just wanted to meet me and to talk. In fact, I don't recall ever meeting a French person who was critical of the stand I was taking. Several of the men I worked with were veterans of their country's ill-fated military adventures in Indochina. They would tell me that the United States was going to lose the war. "We know, we fought there," they would say.

At the end of the workday, we would all shake hands again, say, "À *demain!*" and go our separate ways. Usually I was on my own and lonely. I saw Max and Simone once in a while. There was a woman named Sophie who worked for Simone at the bookstore. She was about thirty, small, dark. I think she was Armenian. We went out a few times. She took me to the flea market and I bought an old French army belt that I kept for years.

Working at the factory was interesting, even enjoyable, and I was learning a lot. In fact a perfect example of how I like to learn. Studying French in a classroom holds no attraction for me at all. But that was a painful time in my life, too. I thought a lot about my family and how hard it must have been for them not to know where I was and how I was doing. Yet, I didn't want to contact them because I was afraid they would tell the authorities where I was. They would think they were doing it for my own good, and possibly out of a sense of patriotic duty. And even contacting my brother Ron would have been risky because there was a good chance the FBI would be monitoring him.

But at the same time I was getting increasingly frustrated because I wasn't doing the antiwar work that I wanted to be doing. Taking the huge decision to leave the Army didn't make much sense if I couldn't work effectively toward stopping the war. When I got my residency papers, the police warned me to stay out of politics. I chose to interpret that to mean I should stay out of French politics, not American politics. So I was itching to get involved again.

Then, one morning in early December, I turned on the radio and heard that Black Power leader Stokely Carmichael was in Paris, although he was having trouble with immigration officials at Orly Airport. The idea hit me: Why not appear at a news conference with Stokely? That would get some attention. Paris was his last stop on a round-the-world speaking tour. the *International Herald Tribune* was full of stories about how much attention his trip was drawing.

So I called Max from the factory office and ran the idea by him. I told him that an American deserter appearing on national TV with Stokely Carmichael would have an impact that would be worth it even if the French government came down on me for it.

We had been talking about organizing with antiwar GIs still inside. So thinking the acronym for Resisters Inside the Army, RITA, was kind of catchy, we would use the news conference to announce that antiwar effort. With his connections, Max had the news conference arranged within hours. It was to be held that night.

Stokely Carmichael was one of the black activists that I had admired since my high school days, along with Martin Luther King. Boxer Cassius Clay (of course later known as Muhammad Ali) was another. While a lot of white people, including my father, took offense at Clay's brazen attitude, I got a kick out of it. I remember how irritated Dad was when I rooted for Clay to beat Sonny Liston. In a way, Muhammad Ali and Stokely Carmichael were cut from the same cloth. They both had an in-your-face, we're-not-going-to-take-it-anymore attitude. Stokely said they were no longer going to ask the white man for equality. "We know we're black. We know we're beautiful," he said. It seemed so positive. It seemed such an affirmation to me. They had eloquent anger. That's how I would describe now what I heard when I saw those guys on TV.

Carefully avoiding the French media, we invited only CBS News, the *New York Times* and a Dutch TV network to the news conference. It was held in an upper floor apartment. I remember how out of breath Stokely was after climbing the stairs and I thought, "Gee, this guy isn't in very good shape." But it was like meeting a boyhood hero nonetheless—not an American League batting champion or a Grand National stock car driver, but someone who was really making a difference.

The apartment living room was divided by a white bed sheet, the news people on one side, Max, Stokely and me on the other. That was to protect Max's anonymity, another of his cloak-and-dagger theatrics.

It took me a while to learn the ways of news people. I spent a lot of time with them in Paris before I realized every word spoken had to be considered first. One time I mentioned as an aside that, just before enlisting in the Army, my girlfriend and I had broken up. I was furious to read a newspaper piece saying I had enlisted because of feeling morose after the breakup.

But that first night I was still pretty innocent about it all. I had given a few interviews from behind a sheet, but that night I stepped around the sheet, sat down at a table before the cameras and microphones and reporters and started talking about being in the Army and growing to oppose the war. It went fairly smoothly for a young guy who had never done anything quite like it. After I finished my statement, Stokely came out from behind the sheet. The two of us answered questions. They asked me what I thought about the Black Power movement. They asked Stokely what he thought of the GI antiwar movement. They asked Stokely about the long trip he was just ending. As I recall, he had been to North Vietnam, North Korea and Sweden, among other places. In Sweden, he had attended a war crimes tribunal. He was tired and seemed distracted when he first arrived at the apartment. But when he stepped in front of the cameras he just clicked in, focused.

Here is how reporter John L. Hess described the interview in the December 10, 1967, edition of the *New York Times*:

> Paris, Dec. 9—A soft-spoken, clean-cut young GI sat before a white screen, gave his name, rank and serial number, and announced that he would not return to duty until the United States got out of Vietnam.
>
> The boy identified himself as Pvt. Richard Perrin, 19 years old, of Springfield, Vt., a tank mechanic in the First Battalion of the 64th Armored Brigade at Kitzingen, West Germany.
>
> Seated between Stokely Carmichael, the Negro nationalist, and an unidentified young Dutch activist, Private Perrin described what he called a growing movement of resistance to the war within the army in the United States, Western Europe and Vietnam.
>
> The midnight interview, filmed by a television crew of the Columbia Broadcasting System, had been arranged in a cloak-and-dagger fashion, with rendezvous in a crowded café, a copy of the *New York Times* as identification, a drive to a middle-class apartment and a voice behind the screen, interrupting questions for security reasons.
>
> The voice, in faintly accented English, required that the time and place of the interview be given only as "recently somewhere in Western Europe."
>
> A dark-haired, dark-eyed youth in a red sweater, clean white shirt and slacks, walked through the screen of bedsheets, sat down before the cameras and began quietly:

"I am Private Richard G. Perrin, RA 11748246. I'm a Rita."

Rita is peace-movement slang for "resist inside the army," the new turn in an effort that previously encouraged GIs to desert. Under questioning the story of how Private Perrin had become a Rita gradually emerged...."

Before Stokely left after the interview that night, he invited me to meet him at a jazz club the next evening. He wanted to rap with me some more without Max and the press around. The club was frequented by American blacks living in France, many of them students. Paris had several clubs like that, featuring jazz, blues, R&B. We had some good times in those places. Many young French people liked the music and the Americans they shared it with.

I went to the club that night with a red-haired American woman whose name I cannot remember. We found Stokely sitting in a corner, holding court. Finally it was my turn to go sit with him. He advised me about how we could work effectively in our exile community. His last piece of advice surprised me. He said to stay away from the communists.

Later, I danced with Stokely's girlfriend, Kathy Simms. She kidded me about how she would have to teach me how to move. The gossip around the place that evening was that Stokely had taken up with Miriam Makeba, who was becoming an international hit, not only for her music, but also bravely speaking out against apartheid in her homeland.

After that night, I spent more time with the black community, including some Black Power rallies. Kathy and her friends tried to teach me how to dance, usually to a Stax-Volt revue album, Carla Thomas inciting us to get our mojos workin'. Sometimes novelist Richard Wright's daughter (I don't remember, was her name Julia?) put in an appearance, but somehow she did not seem to socially be part of the black community in Paris. Either she wasn't given to smiling, as some people aren't, or she was a terribly unhappy person.

All of that was after I got back to Paris, because the day after I met Stokely at the club, Max told me I should get out of town for a while. We weren't sure how the French government would react to the interview. Max had a friend, a member of the

Communist Party, whose brother was a minister in de Gaulle's cabinet and had a mansion outside of Paris that he used only in summer. So that's where we went. Max said if the police were looking for me, they'd never think to look there.

The country house was huge. The living room alone was the size of a two-bedroom bungalow. A massive chandelier hung about twenty feet high, suspended from the ceiling. There was an English woman house-sitting with her child, so I did have some company. We wined and dined together and a couple times she followed me to my bedroom. But, for one of the few times I wasn't interested in getting involved with a woman, even in a casual way. I was preoccupied with politics and worried about how my family was reacting to the interview. And I was tired all the time, emotionally exhausted after those months in Paris and then the interview. I slept twelve or fourteen hours a day and then wandered around country lanes. But I was antsy, bored out of my tree, with no news, no way to know what was going on.

Max came out to visit after about a week. He said everything was cool, but that I should stay another week just to be sure. That was bad news. At night, I could see the lights of Paris glowing in the distance and that's where I wanted to be. And what about my family? That was my main worry.

As might have been expected, while I was hiding out on a country estate, my family was in turmoil. The newspaper clips my Mom saved tell the story. The December 11 *Rutland Daily Herald* (Rutland is in western Vermont, that state's second largest city, not far from Springfield) noted that the news had broken the day before, in the Boston Sunday papers and the *New York Times*. Then there was the CBS telecast Sunday evening, which "used a relatively long film of the boy's parents, bracketed with shots of the interstate highway near Springfield and the neat white house of the Perrin family on Route 106 in North Springfield...." The paper reports that my Dad told CBS in an "emotion-packed" interview: "Our boy was a good quiet boy. He was a good soldier, but he got influenced from outside, by ministers and others from all walks of life."

Our town paper, the *Times-Reporter*, went for the local angle that Monday after the story broke. Reporters talked to some of my high school teachers and concluded that I had been "an average student at Springfield High School, well rounded if not outstanding." The story went on to say: "His interests and concerns led him to emulate his brother in the reading of philosophy and alienated him from his father, a barber in North Springfield who said he couldn't understand the boy."

The paper talked with my social studies teacher, Earl Boudette, who said he "got the impression [Dick] was reading, perhaps beyond his depth. Nietche (sic), for one. I guess he was trying to understand his brother's interests."

Whatever! I was reading hotrod magazines, not philosophy. I may have mentioned my brother's academic interests but they weren't mine.

That theme—that somehow it was all Ron's fault, or the Rev. Henderson's fault, or even Ralph Flanders' fault (he was a U.S. senator at the time)—was echoed in the burst of letters to the editor in newspapers across the state. Other letter writers supported me. One woman from Shaftsbury wrote, "It is unfair not to credit this young fellow with the ability to do his own thinking about this illegal, immoral war declared by one man."

The *Burlington Free Press*, Vermont's biggest newspaper, editorialized about the threat of a racial war in America. It saw my press conference in Paris as an example of the looming menace: "There also was a terribly pathetic story of a Vermont soldier, Pvt. Richard G. Perrin of Springfield, who sat beside Stokely Carmichael at a press conference and called for the defeat of the United States in Vietnam."

A surprisingly sympathetic viewpoint appeared in a December 16 column by the editor of the *Times-Argus* in Barre and Montpelier, the state capital. Of course he, too, was looking for a local angle: "Richard's grandfather, Marius Perrin, came to Barre from France where he had been occupied in the quarrying business. Richard's father is a brother of Marcel Perrin, of the late John Perrin, and of Mrs. Howard McCarthy of Plainfield [actually East Montpelier]. Richard's half-brother, Ronald, of Poway, Calif., is a nephew of Mrs. Harold Waugh of 105 Hill Street, Barre....

"Ronald's mother was Ella Williamson. After her death at 34, Rene Perrin married Betty Hale, a native of Rutland, Vermont, whom he met at the veterans hospital in Rutland, Mass. They were married at the Waugh home, which was then in the house next to the present Ownes store on Washington Street."

That is a local connection all right, except that I know the wedding took place in Rutland, Vermont. In any event, the editor went on to say, "Richard was brought up in a good Christian home and, however wrong he may have been in absenting himself from the army without leave, and appearing in France with Stokely Carmichael to criticize the United States, he shares much the same doubts about the Vietnam War as those expressed by Senators William Fulbright, Eugene McCarthy and Robert F. Kennedy and by many other citizens of prominence in this country.

"Though I share some of the misgivings Richard Perrin has about the Vietnam War, I do not condone his method of dissenting, and I have only pity for Stokely Carmichael who, I'm sure, is doing more damage than good to the righteous cause of American Negroes...."

The next week Max came to bring me back to Paris. It was like being liberated from exile, like returning to heaven or something. I grew to be particularly fond of eating there.

As well as typically French food, I had also taken to eating couscous at several small North African restaurants; it was tasty, nutritious and cheap. There was one restaurant in particular, on a narrow side street near l'Hôtel de Ville. It had maybe six or eight tables and a grubby kitchen. There were always huge kettles of couscous stew simmering on the stove. The washroom was a little closet upstairs. There were no lights. You had to feel your way up the twisting staircase, hope you were aiming in the right direction, and then feel your way back down.

Most of the customers were Arab men. They never took their women out. The only woman was the owner's wife. I was usually the only non-North African there, except when I brought friends to eat with me. The woman and her husband always gave me a warm welcome. In my circle it became known as Dick's couscous restaurant.

A crock of stew and a platter of couscous, all you could eat, along with a liter of Algerian wine, cost about five francs, about a buck U.S. I couldn't eat French food for that, although sometimes I would go to a small French place and order *boudin* (blood sausage). That was another inexpensive meal.

All the music on the jukebox at the couscous restaurant was Arab. After everyone was well fed and liquored, the men would get up and dance together, holding their arms up to their heads and rubbing bellies. It was almost erotic.

There was one guy in particular who didn't have any teeth. The place served little peppers on small plates. The peppers were so hot I couldn't even touch one to my lips. That toothless guy had seen me try to eat them and knew I couldn't do it. He would sit there smiling at me and eat whole peppers one after the other.

Soon after I got back to Paris from the country estate, Max told me that if I went to a certain studio I would be able to watch the piece CBS News put together, just as it had been shown on the air in the States. The film was on a reel, as I recall. That was years before the videocassette recorder.

I sat in a small theater with several people I didn't know and the film began—first my interview and then Stokely's. Then some shots of my hometown in Vermont. That was a shock. There was our family home and the church where Rev. Henderson had preached. Then there was Dad and my sister Nancy sitting on the living room couch and answering questions. I will never forget how upset and burdened my Dad looked. It was clear he was having trouble holding himself together. I was stunned. Some of those watching the film with me laughed at my Dad's comments, but I didn't see any humor in it.

The projectionist asked if I wanted to see the film again. I couldn't speak. I shook my head and walked out, wandered around the city in a near stupor, agonizing over what I had done to my family. It was one of the most difficult moments of my life.

And it hurt me deeply that my Mom and Dad didn't understand what I was doing. But even then my belief in the stand I had taken against the war was strong. I knew it was the right way for me to go and I knew I had to push on.

PARIS 1968

In January 1968, Tian told me his girlfriend would be moving in and I would have to find another place to live. One of Simone's friends, Madame Meyer, had a maid's room available because her maid lived out. However, she wanted to meet me before agreeing to any arrangement, so the three of us had lunch together, Simone, Madame Meyer and I. Madame Meyer thought it would be just fine if I moved in. And so I moved, this time to a pretty swanky part of the city.

The top floor of the building, upstairs from Fauchon, the famous exclusive food store, had eight or so single rooms, most of which were unoccupied. Originally they housed domestic staff, but with changing times there were few live-ins any longer. So the rooms were used for storage or as guest rooms. Most of the time I was alone on the floor.

A narrow, winding stairway climbed the seven stories up from the courtyard, a separate stairway in the back. My new room was directly at the top of the stairs. I walked in and went straight to the window. It latched in the center and opened like a French door, as do most of the windows in that country. I swung it open and looked out upon l'église de la Madeleine. Napoleon and Josephine were married in that church, I was told. And there that magnificent structure was, right outside the window. Madame Meyer asked if the room would do. I said I was very pleased.

The room was about one hundred and twenty square feet, with a single bed, a desk and an armoire. The toilet was across the hall beside the stairway, the kind you stand and squat over. There

82

was a cold-water tap at the end of the hall. But there was no sink. Water ran from the tap to a floor drain. To bathe, I drew water from the tap, heated it in my electric coffee pot, and then poured it into a washbasin on the floor placed on lots of newspapers. With one foot at a time in the basin, I more or less gave myself a sponge bath, the newspapers soaking up the spillage.

I loved my room, but grabbed every opportunity for a shower or real bath. Occasionally the Meyers invited me down for dinner and bath.

The Meyers were Jewish, he a clock manufacturer, she a philanthropist. I noticed that there were numbers tattooed on Madame Meyer's arm, like a serial number on a car. Later, I asked Simone about it and she told me Madame Meyer had survived Auschwitz. What a grim bit of history hitting close to home.

Two teenaged children completed the family. The daughter loved to practice her English on me. She asked me once who my favorite philosopher was. If I recall right she said hers was Spinoza. We didn't have much in common. But I noticed many of the kids I met in France knew a lot about the world, notably more than the young people in North America.

The Meyers were good to me. They let me have my room rent-free for the rest of my stay in Paris. But they were much too cultured and sophisticated for me to feel at ease with them.

Meanwhile, our antiwar group, RITA, was growing. We held a news conference to officially launch it and that attracted some media attention. Our newsletter, *Act* gave American soldiers information about the war and urged them to resist inside the Army. Civilian groups such as the German Students for a Democratic Society and the Dutch Provos helped us to get *Act* into the hands of GIs. Soon we were distributing the newsletter all over western Europe and beyond. We developed a network with soldiers still in the military, guys who wanted to take part but were reluctant to desert. We made a point of saying that was okay. In fact, those antiwar GIs who stayed in became really helpful. One company clerk in West Germany, for example, sent us blank leave forms. With a military ID card and forged leave papers, we could move AWOL GIs from country to country. We never got caught, either.

RITA was but one of many organizations that were doing the same kind of work. Some concentrated their efforts in the United States, some in Vietnam, others in various European countries. Most, but not all, of RITA's work was with soldiers in West Germany. We were willing to work with the other antiwar groups and I'm proud of that. Unfortunately, there was one other group in Paris that declared us to be CIA sponsored. It was called the Second Front and was led by a guy named Arlo. To this day I can't quite figure out what was behind Arlo and others of his ilk. It seemed that all they wanted to do was create problems for our efforts to end the war. Maybe it was another example of how zealots twist things out of reality. Or maybe Arlo was involved with the CIA. Looking back, it seems that nearly everyone was suspicious of others in the movement. Creating that suspicion was a tactic the government used to try to divide and destroy the antiwar movement. In any case, we did not waste any time or energy fighting the Second Front. We kept our arrows aimed at the U.S. government.

When I first arrived in Paris there were a handful of American GIs in my situation and, to be honest, I was not impressed by their motives, which seemed more self-serving than political, or conscientious. But that began to change, however slowly. First Terry Klug and then Phil Wagner arrived and they were people who wanted to do something to bring the war to an end. George Wuerth from the Navy. Many others and I'm sorry that I don't remember names.

Of all the guys involved with RITA, Terry Klug came to be my closest friend. He came to Paris from Italy, where he had been living on the lam. While there, he picked up some work as an extra in the making of the film, *Anzio*. That was a bit of a hoot—an American deserter appearing in a war movie.

Terry was about average in height and slim. No matter what he was doing his look was often cast down, as if he were contemplating something dark. He liked his drink, especially calvados, which a University of Wisconsin professor named Harvey Goldberg supplied him. After a few drinks, Terry would talk of his love for Nina Matchkaloff, his high school sweetheart. That must have frustrated Professor Goldberg.

Terry had an interesting past. His stepfather worked for the United Nations and Terry had lived in several countries when he was a boy. He talked, for example of life in Nicaragua, of how he hunted iguana with a slingshot and particularly how he liked the girls there. That was no surprise. Terry liked girls anywhere. But it was Nina he spoke of most. Years later he found her back in the States and I had to smile when I heard they were together.

A month or two after the Stokely interview, I spent several days filming "a day in the life of a deserter" with a CBS crew. They followed me around Paris, filming my daily routine from the time I got out of bed in the morning, fake yawn and all, to my Metro ride to work, to walking down the boulevard Saint-Michel and eating in a restaurant later in the day. Maybe they picked up on some of my habits. I had become very good at living underground, when I had to do it. Whenever I walked, even if I didn't know where I was, I always walked at a steady, rapid pace and never allowed myself to look around. In restaurants, I always checked for an alternative exit and sat with my back to a wall where I could see the entrances.

Anyway I don't think CBS ever ran the film. But they did pay us several hundred dollars for my acting gig.

One day Max asked me to meet him so I could meet a new soldier who was coming through Holland. The Dutch Provos were helping him to get to Paris from West Germany. The three of us talked quite a bit that evening and I liked the guy. He was black and his name was Clarence Montford.

Clarence and I spent quite a bit of time together for the next few months, doing RITA work and socializing, too. I introduced him to the Black Power people I'd met through Stokely and we went to at least one rally together. He was a laid-back kind of guy, better educated than most of the guys I'd met in the Army.

Then one afternoon Clarence called me at the apartment where we published *Act*. He asked me to meet him at a café just off the Champs-Elysées. I said yes but asked him what he was doing over in that expensive neighborhood. He said he didn't want to talk on the phone.

So I went over there and walked into this classy café and there was Clarence in a suit and tie, all spiffed up with a briefcase at his side and a bottle of champagne on the table. I sat down and

85

asked him how he could afford that place. "Well, the champagne is for you," he said. He knew I liked champagne. Whenever I did a press conference or an interview well, Max's friend June, who I'll write about later, would buy me a bottle of champagne to celebrate.

So Clarence poured the champagne and I asked him what the hell was going on. How could he afford a suit and a bottle of champagne? "Well, Dick, I'm an agent from the Army, from Army Intelligence." He said he had been sent to Paris to infiltrate our organization, find out exactly what we were doing and who our civilian contacts were. "I asked you to meet me here before I leave Paris because I like you," he said. He said he didn't want to see me get hurt and that I should have been more careful about whom I worked with. I still don't know if he said those things out of some kind of personal loyalty because of our friendship or if he was at all sympathetic with the antiwar movement. Maybe both reasons came into play because it was an unlikely gesture for an intelligence agent to make.

Anyway, I didn't believe Clarence at first. I said, "Oh, come on. Knock it off!" He reached down for his briefcase, saying, "Well, okay, if you don't believe me," and there in the briefcase were his travel orders to leave Paris. He was an agent all right. Anger took me. I grabbed the neck of the champagne bottle and was about to hit him but somehow stopped myself. Looking back, I know I was hurt, because I liked and trusted the guy and the hurt surfaced as anger. I walked out and left him sitting there.

But Clarence taught me some things. It was important to be careful about whom you got involved with, yes, but it probably wasn't worth being too paranoid about it, as many people of the Left were, both in France and later in Canada. Clarence infiltrated us and knew a lot about what we were doing and knew many of the civilians we worked with but that didn't affect our operation in the least. It certainly did not slow us down. We simply continued on as if nothing had happened. In fact, Clarence had helped us. He worked with us for months, doing press conferences and writing letters to soldiers still in the Army. I should have sent Army Intelligence a bouquet for assigning him to spy on us.

Finding enough money to keep publishing and distributing *Act* and to feed and house the growing number of deserters was always a problem. The newspaper reporters I'd met asked if we got money from Moscow or Peking or Havana and I got a kick out of that. We had a day-to-day struggle just to eat. *Act* was pretty crude. More money would have helped us make it look more professional.

Max had a "special friend", June, and she tried to help in that regard. (She helped in other ways, too.) She had a large, modern apartment near place Saint-Germain-des-Prés, the apartment where we did much of our work. She clearly came from a privileged background and my impression was that she was trying to find her way through left-wing politics. She had two daughters, Alex and Cora. Alex's father was an actor. Cora was the daughter of symphony conductor René Leibowitz. Alex was a Trotskyite, Cora a Maoist. I had something of a crush on Cora, even though she was too young. Probably it was a good thing it wasn't reciprocal. Cora loved R&B, which drove her conductor father nuts. She was a budding radical.

As far as I could tell, Max spent more time with June than he did with his wife. June traveled frequently and ate well. And she knew people in motion pictures and music. I think she was somehow related to Jane Fonda. Anyway, she made arrangements one evening for Max and me to go to the theater with some people she thought might be able to help us with money. I was there representing the antiwar community of American exiles in Paris. We were going to see a Royal Shakespeare Company production of *A Midsummer Night's Dream*.

June was there with Alex and Cora. At the theater we met three women: Sonja Orwell, the writer George Orwell's widow; Felicia (I think that was her name) Bernstein, wife of the famous composer/conductor Leonard Bernstein; and the actress Jane Fonda. Sonja Orwell had long been a supporter of progressive causes, as I recall, and the Bernsteins were known for their support of civil rights activists. The rumor about Jane Fonda was that she had been hanging out with Vanessa Redgrave and was developing some progressive ideas. Jane had just finished making the movie *Barbarella* and she still had that long mane of bleached-blonde hair. She was wearing a miniskirt and leather boots that came up over her knees.

We watched the play and then drove to a fancy restaurant called Le Calavados, just off the Champs Elysée. The late dinner would give us a chance to talk about our antiwar work. We parked on a narrow street by the restaurant. I stayed back to lock up the car I was riding in and fell behind the others. The doorman stopped me as I tried to enter the restaurant. Eyeing my jeans and sweatshirt he said I was not properly attired. The sweatshirt advertised racing equipment and was left over from my California hot-rodding days. Jane was climbing the stairs to the dining area. I called out to her, told her they wouldn't let me in, and she turned. "Oh, you're with Miss Fonda," the doorman said. "Please come in, monsieur."

At the table, Jane kept looking around to see who was noticing her, much like the young politicians I worked with years later. They usually get over it. Mrs. Bernstein was the most talkative as we dined. I recall that she was quite critical of the piano player in the corner. Sonja Orwell was quieter and warm. I talked about the Vietnam War and the work we were doing in Paris. They asked a lot of questions and all three seemed to be interested and sympathetic, although I don't recall if we got any money from them.

Nor do I recall ever seeing Sonja Orwell or Mrs. Bernstein again, but I did see Jane a few times. Once we went to watch a movie about the war. I brought my Vietnamese friend Tian along. Another time she gave me a box of her husband Roger Vadim's unused clothing to distribute. I kept one shirt for myself. It had a little alligator on it.

One day Jane asked me if I would like to go to a film studio to see a test screening of *Barbarella*. She said to bring a few of our guys along. I brought three. When we arrived, we looked into the small theater and saw several dozen people dressed to the nines. As usual, we were in sweatshirts and jeans. That made me uncomfortable at first. Then Jane spotted me, called out my name, and made a production of coming through the crowd to me. She gave me a hug and a kiss, which wasn't unusual in that set. They hug and kiss even when they don't like each other. But I think Jane was trying to make a statement to them by paying attention to me.

Jane introduced us to Roger Vadim and his son, whose mother was the actress Catherine Deneuve. The boy was overdressed in a burgundy velour suit. He seemed uncomfortable and unhappy with his lot.

We watched the movie, which wasn't remarkable, although I do remember thinking that Jane looked pretty darn good without any clothes on. In the years since, it has been interesting to watch how she changed and changed again from the Barbarella I met in 1968.

RITA had several hideouts. One was at an old farmhouse outside of Tours southwest of Paris. I went there two or three times to drop off or pick up deserters. I remember a big kitchen with a long table that could seat maybe fourteen people comfortably. But the most intriguing aspect of the place was the big yard around the house. It was dotted with crazy constructions that swung in the breeze and moved in nearly every direction. Sometimes the movements were awkward, other times gentle, graceful. I had no name for them because I had never seen a mobile before, nor even heard of one. I certainly didn't have any sense of them as an art form and wouldn't have thought of them that way even after seeing them. But I did find them intriguing.

Our host at the farmhouse was a gentle, quiet man named Sandy. Every time I saw him he was wearing bib overalls. It seemed to me that it was his wife who was the political one of the two. Years later, in 1976, I sat down with my wife Karen in Regina, Saskatchewan to watch the news on TV. On came a story about the death of a famous artist. The name didn't mean anything to me until they flashed a photograph of him on the screen. I jumped out of my chair and said, "Karen, that's Sandy. Sandy Calder!" So, the sculptor Alexander Calder was someone I had worked with in France and I hadn't known he was a famous artist.

.

I was still exchanging letters with my family that late winter and spring. This excerpt from a letter I received from Mom in February shows that we were still a long way apart:

> I have copies of my last two letters to you before me and I can't see what I said to give you the idea that we are "proponents of the war." That is a figment of your imagination. I wrote you last summer that no one thinks war is any more stupid than I [do]. We don't like war but we don't go along with your method of showing your disapproval.

What are you doing that is (in) any way constructive? What a small minority group in Paris or Stockholm or elsewhere is doing isn't going to change the direction of the war—as much as you would like it to. Now you are going to retaliate with "And what are you doing to show your disapproval?" and of course the answer is "We aren't doing a thing." I would rather do nothing than carry on in a destructive manner. I guess we have a little more faith in this country than you do. This country has pulled together when the need was there and it can again. (Don't ask me why it isn't because I don't know.) But what does one gain by running away? Sure you could sell everything and run to Europe but there is no Utopia there anymore than here.

Your statement in the *Reporter* tells "why I resist" but doesn't tell of anything constructive that you are doing about it. We expected an avalanche of letters to the editor and to us, but there were none. I guess that indicates something; perhaps the public has had its fill of the type of Perrin news of late....

I had written a sort of New Year's greeting to the people of Springfield, and the *Connecticut Valley Times-Reporter* published it in the February 8 edition. I told the people I knew they thought I had been brainwashed. "On the other hand," I wrote, "I can't very well take seriously some of your arguments, for I agree with Senator Aiken when he says that you have been duped. [Longtime Vermont Senator George Aiken was an early opponent of the war. With his dry, Yankee humor, he said the smartest course the United States could take would be to declare victory in Vietnam and leave.]

"[President] Johnson says that we're in Vietnam to 'preserve democracy for the Vietnamese.' Can you really accept this? Does it look like that is what we're doing?

"What we are really saying is that we will give democracy to the Vietnamese even if we have to kill every last one of them to do it.

"Who is running the war? And who is running the 'democratic process' of our country?"

I went on to point out that corporations such as Boeing and Dow Chemical were finding the war profitable. Among the presidential possibilities in that year's election, only Eugene McCarthy would have done "anything to change our insane foreign policy" and, without the backing of big business, he didn't stand a chance. That was the gist of my statement. My Mom said in that same letter that Aiken had written to them recently and, judging from his tone, "He doesn't think your actions are in the best interests of your country any more than I do."

I had already written to my family earlier that month, noting that, as far as the press was concerned, I was already "rather old hat," but that I had accepted a speaking invitation in Tours and turned one down for a big rally in Berlin, because it was too risky to go back into Germany.

Mom's next letter dated April 1 was filled with family news, but she did mention Johnson's announcement that he was not going to seek reelection. "Maybe, in time, we will see some changes in current trends, which can scarcely be anything but better," she wrote. She mentioned Robert Kennedy's stepping quickly into the political vacuum, and there was hope in that for some people, but we all remember how that turned out, some of us with an inner twist of real tragedy and sense of loss. But, as I wrote to my Mom in early April, I was still supporting Eugene McCarthy's presidential bid. She urged me to write to my sister Nancy, so I did. It was mostly a big-brother letter meant to break the ice, but it also lamented the loss only the day before of Martin Luther King. I reminded her of the march we attended together with Ron that summer in Chicago.

Meanwhile, my life in Paris went on. And there were some lighter moments. One day, some while after I moved out of Tian's apartment, he invited me back for a party. Most of the guests were French students, but there was one young English woman. She sat on the stool by Tian's grand piano. Her miniskirt was so short that it didn't even reach the stool. She had great legs and turned out to be an incorrigible tease. Guy after guy hit on her, but she rejected them all. I remember thinking, though, that there was something vulgar in the clothing of a lot of the English women who came around. The French women I knew were more modest dressers. But, vulgar or not, those French guys were hitting on her. And so was I.

And there were moments that weren't so light. Riding home late one night on the métro, I was alone with a couple who were arguing in a language that wasn't French. Maybe Portuguese.

The man started beating on the woman. They were both small and both drunk. After a short while of trying to ignore them, I felt I had to do something. I approached the man from behind and grabbed his arms. The woman started yelling and screaming at me and then began hitting me with her purse. I let the man go and went back to my seat and he went back to hitting her. I got off at the next stop and walked home.

I should have learned then, that you can't help someone who doesn't want to be helped. I didn't and it has caused me considerable grief since.

Some would agree that our dominant culture and its victims need help as badly as the woman on the métro. I have seen some lifelong political activists become disenchanted and sometimes quite bitter that humanity hadn't come to understand, let's say, that war is a dead-end, or that the environmental mess we're creating will in itself be a dead-end.

We sure need to hear the voices of the concerned. They should go into it understanding that though society needs to be fixed, an intransigent population can't be helped any more than the woman on the metro. People, as long as they're comfortable, generally don't want to recognize the mess about them. They won't want real remedy until they are hurting enough. Someday! La lutte continue!

During the Vietnam War, I don't think comfortable America heard the antiwar movement until the Kent State students were murdered by National Guardsmen.

Again on a lighter note, I met a young American couple just arrived in Paris, graduate students as I recall. They invited me to their place for dinner. I looked over the record albums they had brought with them. One cover showed Frank Zappa sitting on a toilet. What in the world was this? I left the States in the summer of '67 and missed the emergence of acid rock. There was a bit of it around before I left, I guess. I remember the Jefferson Airplane, but at the time I didn't like it. There was a big change in the North American youth culture in the year-and-a-half I was gone.

I did like rhythm and blues and the French knew all about that. They loved Aretha Franklin and the Temptations. Christian, the apprentice at the envelope factory, was the one who told me Otis Redding had died.

In a letter dated May 12, Mom reminded me that Ron was coming to Europe soon and asked if I wanted him to bring any of my clothes. But by then the events of May—sparked in part by the student confrontation with police at the Sorbonne that I described in the first chapter—were on and I doubt that I ever answered the letter. Its pastoral tone contrasted wildly with the insurrection I had been swept into as Paris erupted night after night.

Dad and me at his Rutland barber shop circa 1954.

That's me in uniform...taken at Fort Gordon, Georgia.

Relaxing on my bunk at Fort Leonard Wood, Missouri, 1967.

My barrack at Fort Sill with baseball field in foreground.

With Terry Klug on the right...taken in Paris, 1968.

My French carte de sejour.

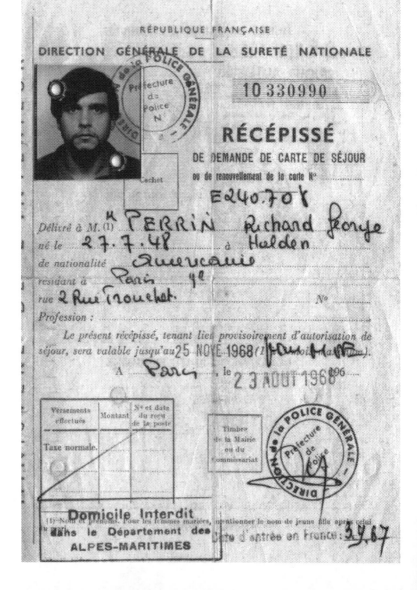

Being interviewed with Stokely Carmichael at a RITA press conference in Paris, 1967.

Clarence Montford in Paris, 1968.

With Tommy and Irma Douglas, 1983.

Dad and Mom lobbying for amnesty Rep. James Jeffords (R.) of Vermont. Now Senator, Jeffords is the man who recently tipped the balance of power in Washington.

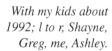

With my big brother, Ron, in 1985.

With my kids about 1992; l to r, Shayne, Greg, me, Ashley.

*In the speaker's chair,
House of Commons,
Ottawa, 1989.*

*With my 50th birthday
project, 1948 Chev
pickup.*

LANGUEDOC 1968

The students' revolutionary strategy was clear from the beginning. Provocation, usually by a militant minority, would be followed by government repression, which would generate popular support for the revolutionaries. For a few weeks in May, it worked. Daniel Cohn-Bendit, who was only twenty-three, spelled it out in an interview with Jean-Paul Sartre in the May 20 edition of *Le Nouvel Observateur*. He said bluntly that bourgeois society would not be toppled in one push. It would take a series of revolutionary shocks. It was the role of the activist minority to detonate those shocks and establish a process of change. Spontaneity was the strength of the movement, Cohn-Bendit said. Students could set the pace, he said, but they would eventually have to merge with the workers in combat against the state.

By the time the events of May broke out, the student groups involved were already far to the left of the French Communist Party, which did its best to distance itself from them. The French party was still doggedly loyal to the Soviet Union, but Moscow was no longer the focus of the left-wing youth movement. As it was in most western countries, the new focus was on the third world, and especially the war in Vietnam. Opposing American imperialism in Vietnam was in part an inflammatory symbol for the global class struggle as a whole. Opposing the Vietnam War became the common revolutionary coin of the West. That, of course was altogether compatible with RITA's agenda.

All of this had been building for at least eighteen months before I found myself that May in the courtyard of the Sorbonne

94

that I described in the first chapter. What I didn't tell you about that day, because the professor whisked me out of the police line and I was not arrested, I have had to piece together from later reports.

Although the students surrendered peacefully after the police burst through the courtyard doors, many of them were herded out and loaded onto the black police vans parked on the street outside the university walls. A crowd of students had gathered nearby. The students watched as the police vans began to move away, knowing their comrades were packed in those black boxes like slaves on a ship. Shouts and jeers went up as outrage swept the crowd. The students surged forward and pounded their fists on the vans. Someone threw a stone. And then another. One stone shattered a police windshield, bloodying the driver. Cars were overturned to block the police caravan. Police lobbed teargas grenades. In those few minutes, the pattern of the May rebellion that I described earlier was set.

While I escaped through that side door of the Sorbonne and tried to make myself scarce, the police were on a rampage. They beat everyone in sight, rebels and innocent onlookers alike, all in a choking fog of teargas.

Ironically, on that day, May 3, 1968, Paris was chosen to host the Vietnam peace talks.

But that ferocious police repression generated a unity among the students that probably nothing else could have achieved. Within twenty-four hours, students all over the country—from Montpellier to Caen, Grenoble to Toulouse—had joined the rebellion with strikes and demonstrations. During those first days of the rebellion, students all over France, including high schoolers, exploded in a burst of revolutionary joy. Suddenly it seemed that anything was possible.

A poll taken on May 8 indicated that about 80 percent of Parisians supported the students. A group of well-known intellectuals, including Jean-Paul Sartre and Simone de Beauvoir, sent de Gaulle a telegram appealing for student amnesty and a reopening of the university. There was no response. Later in the month Sartre appeared at the Sorbonne and drew an overflow crowd, even though many of the students looked upon him (at age sixty-three) as an old man. Although Herbert Marcuse (the

95

philosopher Ron was studying with in San Diego) was heralded as the theoretical guru of the student movement, Cohn-Bendit admitted that few French students had read Marcuse while nearly all had read Sartre. The "old man's" support meant a lot to them.

Meanwhile events were building towards what became known as "The Night of the Barricades," May 10-11. It began in the afternoon of May 10, not with seasoned police agitators, not with left-wing organizers or even university activists, but with about five thousand high school students marching near Montparnasse and calling for the release of their comrades who had been detained earlier. Before long they were joined by older protesters and the crowd swelled to about fifteen thousand. As a conciliatory gesture, the government offered to withdraw the police from the Latin Quarter and to allow the Sorbonne to reopen. But it was too late. The crowd's blood was surging and marchers kept calling for the release of their comrades.

Leaders tried to guide the crowd across the Seine to the state broadcasting system building on the Right Bank, but police blocked the bridges and forced the protesters back onto their own Left Bank territory around the university. By about nine that evening the first barricade, for the most part comprised of overturned automobiles, had gone up. To avoid violence, the rector of the Sorbonne tried to negotiate with student leaders Alain Geismar and Daniel Cohn-Bendit, but the two sides were at loggerheads. The university was unable to meet student demands for freedom and amnesty for all arrested students and the removal of the police from the Latin Quarter. Cohn-Bendit emerged from the talks and announced that they had told the rector "what was happening in the street tonight is a whole generation rising against a certain sort of society. We told him blood would flow if the police did not leave the Latin Quarter." (Quoted in *French Revolution* 1968 (London: Heinemann/Penguin, 1968), from which a lot of this information is taken.) And blood was shed.

Shortly after one in the morning, the university announced that the talks had collapsed and an hour later the police attacked. Once again the air swirled with tear gas as we fought the attackers hand-to-hand until well after dawn. By the end of that battle there were sixty or more barricades in the Latin Quarter, many of them constructed of paving stones ripped from the street in traditional French revolutionary fashion.

Curiously, both the French and the American republics emerged from revolution—and at about the same time—the American Revolution beginning in 1776 and the French in 1789. The French had to make several goes at it before they won a republic that lasted, and that long experience left them with a revolutionary spirit that is still never far beneath the surface. That spirit is not there in most Americans, possibly because the nation developed from such a mélange of cultures, more intent on commerce than on the common man.

By the time that Cohn-Bendit went on the air at 5:30 that morning of May 11 and ordered the rebels to disperse, there were hundreds of casualties (luckily, no one was killed) and hundreds of protesters arrested. Property damage was extensive.

Luckily for him (and perhaps the de Gaulle government), Prime Minister Georges Pompidou was out of the country when the violence intensified that night. He returned the evening of May 11 and, having had no direct hand in the police repression, was able to become the voice of conciliation. He announced that the Sorbonne would be allowed to reopen the next Monday and implied that the rest of the student demands would be met. But it was too late. The revolutionary momentum could not be appeased. Outraged by the police repression, the country's two largest trade unions called for a general strike on Monday, May 13. The teachers' federation joined in. Some individual workers had joined the barricades earlier, but with that strike call the link between the students and the workers was completed.

On Monday the country was paralyzed, factories still, public services frozen. Led by Geismar, Cohn-Bendit and other student leaders, a massive crowd of about eight hundred thousand students and workers marched through the streets, banners streaming. It was an overwhelming thing to see and be part of. The demonstration ended at the Sorbonne. Pompidou had kept his word and reopened the gates. Students stormed in and claimed the university as if it were a captured town. On Tuesday, workers all over France followed the students' example and began occupying their factories while refusing to work. From mid-May to mid-June about ten million workers were involved and that was something the government could not ignore. Student uprisings had been more or less sloughed off in countries around the world that year, including the United States, but only in France did the workers become involved and, with the country's economy under siege, attention had to be paid.

De Gaulle returned from an ill-timed trip to Romania and as the days passed his government began to take a tougher line. Noting that Cohn-Bendit was out of the country speaking to other student movements, the government banned him from returning to France. French students were enraged. In Paris and elsewhere, the fighting went on night after night, as I described earlier. There was savage fighting on the night of May 24. A policeman was killed in Lyons and a young rebel in Paris. Pompidou accused the rebels of trying to ignite a civil war. He was struggling to negotiate an agreement with the trade unions and they came up with a deal to end the strikes, but the workers would have none of it.

Demonstrations had been banned, but on May 27 the students called for a mass meeting at a Paris soccer stadium. At least 35,000 students showed up. I don't know why, but I was not there. Overshadowed for a time by the government-trade union negotiations, the students now regained the lead and the workers were at their side. It seemed for a moment that the revolutionary pieces had fallen into place.

But that was when de Gaulle made his move. On the morning of May 29 he cancelled his weekly cabinet meeting. Shortly before noon he left the palace with his wife, ostensibly to travel to their country home at Colombey-les-Deux-Églises. Then he disappeared until evening, bent on a whirlwind effort to rally his troops in eastern France and Baden-Baden, Germany. It's been said that he was prepared to move against Paris militarily if necessary. By the time his helicopter set down in Colombey that evening, the old general, whom nearly everyone thought was finished, was back in charge, although the leaders of the left, poised to take over his government, didn't know it yet.

The next afternoon, Thursday, DeGaulle went on the air and barked out his strategy. In an address lasting less than five minutes, he bashed the "communists" who were trying to take over the country, said his cabinet would be reshuffled, the National Assembly dissolved and called for a general election. I listened to that address and I remember thinking how movingly effective he was when he finished with, "Vive la France, Vive la République." The Paris bourgeoisie, most of which had been cowering before the student-worker onslaught, stormed onto the Champs-Ellysée. The "Marseillaise" replaced the "Internationale" as the crowd marched. Some of the braver in that crowd came over to the Left Bank and there was hand-to-hand fighting on boulevard Saint-Germain. We chased them out. It was almost a month before the Gaullists triumphed in the general election, but on that day, May 30, the revolution that never quite was was over.

The next day the police began to crack down hard. There were reports of troop movements around Paris. Students and workers continued to demonstrate, but we were now pretty much on the run. On June 10, the day the election campaign opened, a high school boy was drowned in the Seine while fleeing police. His death sparked another night of fierce fighting in Paris. Police stations were attacked. The next morning a worker was gunned down after riot police were called in to a Peugeot factory. His death triggered yet another student demonstration in Paris and that led to another brutal night of combat. But the student cause was lost. The next day all demonstrations were banned until the election.

Suddenly leftist expatriates were being arrested and some of them deported, including some Americans who had been in France since the Joseph McCarthy communist witch-hunt in the 1950s. What really alarmed me was when a couple of Spaniards were deported back to Spain. Veterans of the Republican side in the Spanish Civil War, they had been living in France since 1939. They fought with the French resistance during World War II and received the croix de guerre, France's highest military honor, for their heroic actions against the Nazi occupation. Once back in Spain they were immediately arrested.

Incidents of that kind sent a chill through all of us in RITA. There was no telling what the French government would do. The German SDS students were deported after my close call in their apartment where I hid from the police on the closet shelf. Max told me it would be better if I left Paris and laid low for a while.

By then Ron and Sandra and Sasha were in Europe. They had a new Volkswagen camper waiting for them when they arrived and were staying with Tim and Jeannine in Heiligkreuzsteinach. I took the train to Strasbourg and met the five of them there, along with the two dogs, Erich and Clea. Tim and Jeannine were in the baby blue Fiat that had carried me into France. We drove a few miles south to Colmar and stopped at the museum there. Tim told us it was the home of the famous Grünewald crucifixion triptych and he would never go through Colmar without stopping to look at it.

In a town outside of Colmar, I tried to get a hotel room using Tim's passport. My papers had expired. There was a vague resemblance between us, but that didn't fool the woman at the desk. She was immediately suspicious and called the police. No one was taking chances in those unsettled days. We hightailed it out of there and headed southwest toward the Languedoc region, where Sandra's parents lived. The countryside was strikingly peaceful after those violent weeks in Paris.

Sandra's parents lived on a small farm a few kilometers from the village of Bellegarde outside of Toulouse. Their house was hardly more than a peasant hut. A doorway led directly from the kitchen into the stable. There was no indoor toilet. The rooms were small, cramped with the stuff of two long lifetimes. Not much daylight made it inside. There was a radio in one room and at least once a day Ron and Tim and I would gather around it and listen for the news from Paris.

Sandra's mother, Josephine, was small, bent and gnarled. At that point in her life, she could have stepped out of any number of 17th or 18th century paintings of middle European peasants. Her father, Constantin, was slender and erect beneath his floppy straw hat. After a life in exile as a chemical engineer, he spent most of the days of his retirement painting. Some of his pictures had been sold. There was a touch of quixotic madness about him that made him an interesting fellow to be around. We would sit under a cherry tree in the yard and Constantin would tell us tales of Russia and the political adventures of his youth.

Except for the cows his wife milked, they did not work the farm themselves. They rented the fields to the monks in the monastery on the hill. We spent most of a day in that monastery, listening to chant, inspecting their artifacts, sampling their jams and breads and wine.

One afternoon Ron and Tim and I hiked into the village of Le Castera to deliver something to an old friend of Sandra's. The woman was gracious and hospitable. We sat at her big dining room table and drank a glass of wine. After we left her house, we stopped at a small wine cellar on the square and drank some more. Hiking back on the narrow asphalt road between rolling wheat fields beneath a hot sky, we broke into an old French marching song that Tim taught us. *"Un kilomètre à pied"* we bellowed at the top of our lungs, marching arm-in-arm for verse after verse, increasing the kilometers with every verse. There were moments when Paris seemed far away, an impossible place.

Another day, Erich the dog had stretched his big body on the floor by the kitchen stove. Someone spilled boiling water on him. He yowled and raced out the door, plunged into the small pond not far from the house. It was a while before we could coax him out of there. He was burned badly and we had to take him to a vet.

After about a week, Tim and Jeannine left for Béziers, where Jeannine had a job interview at a Texas Instruments plant. (After two days of interviews, including an interview with Tim on the second day, Jeannine got the job. But then they both decided she shouldn't take it. Although the company was American, the management style was decidedly French, too rigid and formal for someone who was used to working with Americans.)

We met Tim and Jeannine at their hotel in Béziers. On the way, we visited the old walled city of Carcassone then stopped in a vineyard for lunch. I don't know how it happened but somehow I left my suitcase there. I didn't notice it was missing until after we met Tim and Jeannine. The next day I had Ron drive me back to get it. Roger Vadim's shirt that Jane Fonda had given me was in that suitcase and I didn't want to leave that shirt behind. When you are not quite twenty years old, you can go through a revolution and still worry about the damnedest things.

That night we camped on the Mediterranean near the small port city of Sète. It was after dark when we got there and we drove into some private property by mistake. We pulled up in a swirl of dust by the rail fence around some sort of resort built to resemble a town in the American wild west. Two men descended on us, both of them dressed in western duds. Tim tried to talk with them but they were belligerent. The short guy said he was the owner and demanded to know why we were trespassing. He was standing by the front fender of the Fiat, just out of the glow of Tim's headlights. Tim said later that he was more worried about the big guy standing by his rear door. A woman came running down from one of the buildings and started talking to Jeannine. She was the owner's wife. Jeannine explained that we were looking for a place to camp. Tim turned his attention to the woman and ignored the men. The owner stuck his thumbs in his big belt and in his best John Wayne voice said, *Quand je pose une question, je demande une réponse.* Tim said he had all he could do to keep from laughing. Things were tense for a few moments, but the woman finally mollified her husband. She said there was a small cove nearby where we could camp. Tim got directions and we beat it out of there.

The cove turned out to be a delight. There was a stretch of beach and we had the place to ourselves. We went skinny dipping in the sea and Sandra cooked a marvelous meal. She had shopped at the fish market in Sète that afternoon. One thing I remember in particular was a shellfish called a *couteau* (razor clam) because its shell was long and boney like the handle of some knives. You squeezed the shell and sucked the living meat as it emerged like toothpaste from a tube. I could feel it wriggling in my mouth before I swallowed it. Sandra liked all kinds of bizarre food and I was game to try anything.

Those were marvelous days by the sea, but Tim and Jeannine had to get back to Germany and, from what we heard on the radio, things had cooled off in Paris. So it was time to go back. No one had called a halt to the carnage in Vietnam while I was away, so I still had a lot of work to do. But I remember that trip to Languedoc as an interlude that was both peaceful and fun and I was sorry to see it end.

PARIS ENCORE   1968

The Events of May combined with my other political activity took so much of my time that I lost my job at the envelope factory. I found a job at a big electrical appliance store called FNAC (I took over the job after another RITA, Philip Wagner, left for Canada) on the boulevard de Sebastapol located in Les Halles, the old market area where so many people ended up slurping onion soup after a night on the town. That was a wonderful area—crowds of people, little streets teeming with trucks. Les Halles, which no longer exists, was a wholesale market. Early every morning the trucks would come in from the countryside with their loads of produce, dairy products and meats and unload them. Then the retailers swarmed in to buy food for their stores and restaurants.

Working at FNAC may well have been one of the best jobs I've ever had. The store sold everything from refrigerators to stereos. My job was to stock beverages into the two canteens, one for the customers and the other for the employees, along with a little cleaning, too. Every day after I stocked the canteens, I took a cart and pulled it through the market, buying soft drinks, juices, beer and wine for the next day.

FNAC's owner had left-wing sympathies. He liked to hire leftist political refugees from countries around the world. I was the only American, the second one to be there, after Philip. There were many Algerians, revolutionaries who had fallen into disfavor after Houari Boumediene came to power in 1965. How things can change. The same people who fought to overthrow French colonial rule in Algeria ended up exiled in France.

There were also several Spaniards working at the store, Republicans still living in exile nearly thirty years after the end of the Spanish Civil War. Our trade union was the Confédération général du travail, which was aligned to the Communist Party. Every morning before the store opened, the intercom was turned on and we all sang a rousing chorus of the communist anthem the "International". I never did learn the words in English, but I know them in French.

It was a curious time for me. On the one hand, I was in the middle of things; on the other hand, I was pretty much out of it. Early that summer, for example, I was walking down the street and a big English headline on a French tabloid caught my eye: "Goodbye Bobby." I thought, "What the hell is that?" and went over to have a look. Bobby Kennedy had been assassinated immediately after he won the California primary in his ill-starred bid for the Democratic presidential nomination.

Somehow that reminds me of how I learned of Che Guevara's death while having a shit in the stand-up toilet across the hall from my room. I used newspapers for toilet paper and sometimes read stories before wiping my butt. (Jeez, I must have had strong legs.) And there it was: "Che Guevara killed in Bolivia."

One of the big topics that summer was the reform effort of the Alexander Dubcek government in Czechoslovakia. We talked about it every day at FNAC. Everyone wondered what the Soviets were going to do. You can imagine how upset we all were when the Soviet tanks rumbled into Prague that August and crushed the reform movement.

Wandering Les Halles with my little cart, I came to know some of the hookers who worked there. They serviced the truckers who came in from the countryside every day. Most of them were middle-aged women, between forty and fifty. All of them had huge breasts bulging out of low-cut striped jerseys right out of the movie *Irma La Douce*. Sometimes I'd stop and have coffee with them. One day as I was wheeling my cart along, one of them pointed out the big red pimple I had on the end of my nose and said to the others, *"Regardez le petit bouton." Petit bouton* (little button) was the hookers' nickname for me from then on. (If there was a racy double entendre there, it escaped me at the time.)

It was interesting to watch the hookers in Paris, to note how even they divided themselves into social (or at least business) classes. The Les Halles hookers were past their prime and near the bottom of the ladder. In an area near where I lived, the Madeleine, there was a side street called rue de Sèze that angled off toward the Opera. That was where the classier hookers sat in sports cars, with their skirts hiked up to their crotch. Men walked up and down the street peering into the cars. If they liked what they saw, they got in and presumably went off to an apartment or room somewhere.

Then, a little further along, near the Olympia Theater, the hookers stood along the sidewalk. They were a step down from the sports car class. I used to chat with them on my way to work at five in the morning to catch the first Métro at the Opera, but I never talked with the hookers in the sports cars. Every morning one or another of the hookers would ask me if I wanted to sleep with them and every morning I would turn them down. I couldn't have afforded it even if I had wanted to.

I bought a packet of ten Métro tickets a week and was careful about how I used them. Every morning I took the Métro to work because it was so early, but I walked home in the afternoon. My work hours were from six to noon, so I had afternoons free. I would walk home, get cleaned up, then go about my political work. In the evening, I headed to the couscous restaurant or maybe to the Tunisian deli on rue de la Huchette, just off place Saint-Michel. That deli served the best sandwich I have ever eaten, bar none. I couldn't afford to eat in the district where I lived. There was a small green space with a park bench not far from the Tunisian place. It was in front of the famous bookstore Shakespeare and Company. What a great place to sit and eat those Tunisian sandwiches while enjoying a view of Notre Dame cathedral on its island in the Seine!

Despite the disruptions of May, our antiwar group RITA was still running smoothly. As I mentioned earlier, our newsletter *Act*, was giving American soldiers information about the war and urging them to resist.

A number of people helped us in those days. I remember Bob Rosen, for example. He was from Columbia University, I think. He liked to meet with me and talk about what I read and heard. (It occurs to me that many of the people who helped through those years were Jews. Were they willing to stick their necks out because of their own relationship to persecution?) I corresponded with Bob for some time after he returned to New York but lost touch with him after a while.

Then there was Austryn Wainhouse. He was a writer and translator who lived in the south of France. As I recall, he was best known for translating the Marquis de Sade's works for Penguin Books. When he visited Paris he would take us to a fine restaurant where we would wine and dine and have stimulating conversations.

I also received a totally unexpected letter of support, the only one I ever received, from a high school classmate, Nola Yasinsky. She was living in Washington D.C. at the time, as I recall and she got my address from Arthur Wright, the editor of the Springfield newspaper. I replied to her letter, but I never heard from her again until I saw her at our high school reunion in 1996. She lives in Africa now.

Sometimes we would get word from the German SDS or the Dutch Provos that an American soldier had left the Army. They would bring the soldier to Strasbourg just across the Rhine from West Germany. After getting out of work at noon, I'd catch the first afternoon train to Strasbourg and spend the evening, usually over a meal, counseling soldiers. Then I would catch the midnight train back to Paris, which would get me there in time to start work at FNAC.

I enjoyed those trips to Strasbourg. Even though it is in France it was like traveling to another country. I hadn't had time to appreciate it when I passed through there after fleeing Paris late in the spring. The German influence in that region, the Alsace, is deep. So the beer was good and the sauerkraut first-rate. And I had a chance to talk with guys who were still in the Army.

One of those trips didn't turn out so well, however. The SDS said they were bringing a soldier who wanted to meet me. I left Paris after work and we met in a restaurant, a couple of German guys, this soldier and me. Early in the conversation, the soldier commented about how great it was that the nigger troublemaker (Martin Luther King) had been eliminated. That was only a short time after King's assassination. I was infuriated and asked him why in the world he wanted to leave the Army. Was he opposed to the war in Vietnam or what?

He said he had trouble working with blacks, especially taking orders from black NCOs and officers. I was disgusted with the guy and told the Germans I didn't want to have anything to do with him. "Get this fucker back across the bridge. I don't want anything to do with him," I said.

But the Germans didn't take him back across the Rhine. They got help from the other group in France, which by that time was calling itself the American Deserters Committee. It was the same group I mentioned earlier, then called the Second Front and headed by a guy named Arlo. Sometime later I ran into that racist soldier in Paris. I was not impressed with the American Deserters Committee for helping him out. But there were lots of things they did that didn't impress me. During the Events of May, for example, the committee issued a press release calling for the overthrow of the de Gaulle government. That was stupid (or maybe a subversive ploy designed to discredit the whole deserter operation in France). Many of us were out there fighting on the barricades, but our position there was too tenuous to be sticking our necks out publicly. The guys who operated the deserters committee were American university students studying in Paris who saw fit to establish their own organization to help deserters. They didn't have their own necks in jeopardy. I guess they didn't think RITA was revolutionary enough, or else they were trying to undermine us with their irresponsible tactics. As I said earlier, they claimed we were a CIA front organization. That may well have been a case of the pot calling the kettle black.

That July, around the first anniversary of my court-martial at Fort Sill, I wrote my father a quarrelsome and somewhat bitter letter. I berated him for refusing to understand what I was trying to do, for telling the world that I had been brainwashed, for coercing me into apologizing to my commanding officer at Fort Sill, making "me crawl on my belly like a dog begging forgiveness" so that he (my father) "could go home feeling better."

But there was something else in that letter, an ambivalence toward what I was doing that documents the way my thinking had been changing in those months. I wrote that in the last three months I had changed my mind and realized that I had not done the right thing when I deserted to France: "In order to work against the war with maximum efficiency I should have stayed with the GIs who go to fight in Vietnam. However I have reached this conclusion after six months of ideological study and thought. In more practical terms, to execute my ideas, being in the Army would be tactically and strategically more effective. I make up for this shortcoming by working with the RITA movement...." Obviously, I was somewhat confused and frustrated. I know I wanted to do the right thing and do it effectively. Now, looking back, I think the Army would have simply kept me locked up in a cell and that is why I left.

Toward the end of the letter, which was dated July 22, I said I was feeling "only desperation with our relationship. I would like it to be better but it is up to you. I will never crawl again, not for anyone."

My father responded almost at once. He said he was wrong to encourage me to join the Army. He said he was wrong to make me apologize to my commanding officer at Fort Sill. "I can understand now why you were so mixed up," he wrote. "I am myself like many other people in this country."

But he insisted that deserting the Army had been a mistake: "You have the right to think the way you want to, Dick, and I can agree with a lot of what you say. But I cannot tell you that you were right leaving the Army. Someday you may learn that you were wrong. And I wouldn't want you to say that I was wrong again."

As I had written him earlier, I was thinking pretty much the same thing, but for different reasons. Terry Klug and I had talked about returning to the Army. Our intent was to get back in so we could work directly with other soldiers and we were naïve enough to think the Army might let us do that.

The police were giving us a hard time when we went to renew our residency papers. The government policy was much stricter since the Events of May. Any foreigner engaging, or even appearing to engage in political activity the French government didn't like was deported. The policy was enforced by the DST (Direction de la surveillance du territoire), which was roughly equivalent to the CIA except that it had a strong domestic arm.

So I would go with my papers to the prefecture at the appointed time and they would make me wait for hours. Then they would grill me for hours more. And every time they would shorten the period until next renewal. I was getting very nervous. By the time October came around I had had enough of it and decided to leave France.

Terry went to the U.S. embassy and said that we wanted to negotiate a return. The Pentagon flew an officer to Paris and we arranged a meeting. We didn't tell anyone about our plans to meet with the officer.

The apartment where the three of us met that evening was on a side street near the Tuileries, not far from my place at the Madeleine. The officer offered us a drink and within minutes Terry went to sleep. He was quite a drinker and there was no way a few sips of one drink could have put him out.

While Terry slept, the officer and I talked. He knew the names of many of the people who worked with us. I guess Clarence Montford had done his work well. I outlined our position: we wanted to return to the Army with no charges against us.

His counterproposal offered an honorable discharge and a ticket home for all the information we had on antiwar activities involving the U.S. military. He, too, seemed to believe that we were receiving help from other governments. He asked me about it several times. It was hard not to laugh. Hell, I didn't have enough money to replace my worn-out underwear. "How can you move people from country to country without foreign assistance?" he asked. I just smiled and thought of the company clerks who supplied us with the documents we needed.

Terry woke up after a while and, unable to negotiate a satisfactory return, we left. But Terry kept insisting that he wanted to go back to the United States. Not I. There was no way I was going to take a chance on doing more stockade time. Terry did go back eventually and he ended up serving a year in the federal prison in Leavenworth, Kansas.

During those months, I was keeping up a fairly frequent correspondence with my family. In a letter to Mom and Dad dated September 2, I was incensed about the Soviet crackdown in Czechoslovakia:

Well, the situation in Prague is very disheartening. I was excited about the prospects of a good system there, so much so that I had given living there a thought. I must condemn the Soviet Union for its military intervention but at the same time I think we must keep in mind the number of times the U.S. has done exactly the same thing; and I might add with a much larger loss of life. Last night I spoke with an American girl who was in Prague at the time of the invasion. I was quite surprised to hear her say she felt safer in Prague than she did at the big antiwar demonstrations in Oakland a few years ago. According to her, the Russian soldiers didn't want to be in Czechoslovakia and it was evident by their facial expressions; whereas the cops in California really acted and looked like they wanted to hurt people. So I will still maintain that rightists are much more inhumanly aggressive than the left. In fact, although aggressive the left isn't inhuman. When the war is over, I bet the American war prisoners will not have much complaint about the way Hanoi treated them....

That last comparison between the political right and left shows how an ideological bent can lead, at the very least, to faulty political analysis. Ideology is dangerous on whatever side. But I was young and still trying to learn. I went on to lecture my parents about how the American people were not living up to their democratic responsibilities by failing to call the government to account: "If you were to read some Jefferson or Paine, you could see that our country isn't what our founders meant it to be. Probably because of some missing elements in their philosophy. Their philosophy certainly has succeeded in some aspects. The U.S. is the richest most powerful empire in all history, but many people are still suffering. People suffer because there are some things lacking in the American way, so we must fill up the gaps."

I ended the letter saying I had read in the *Herald Tribune* that "my generation is the most romantic in history. Maybe that's what I'm all about. Just in love with everything."

My mother responded at the end of September. She said she had spent the day making spiced tomato with my grandmother and passed along a lot of other family news. My father and brother David had closed up the summer camp on Lake Hortonia for the season, "concluding 15 years of summers" there. That is the same camp where Tim McCarthy and I met in the summer of 1996 to go over material for this book.

But my mother also showed a growing political awareness: "H.H.H. (Democratic presidential candidate Hubert Humphrey) is at this moment giving a 'Major Political Speech.' He promises to end the war in Vietnam as soon as possible by honorable means (if elected). I suppose the catch to that statement is 'by honorable means.' Eisenhower made the same promise in regard to Korea and kept his promise. Let's hope H.H.H. might do likewise. And when the war is over, and it will be, we have a problem with us that will be longer than any war, that of the races."

About a week later I responded:

> I went to a Humphrey rally a few nights ago. Pierre Salinger, President Kennedy's press secretary spoke and answered, or rather tried to answer, questions [from] a predominantly young audience. He was a complete failure as far as Humphrey's campaign is concerned. He probably lost more votes than he expected to gain. He spoke about the lesser of two evils bit. The same line as in '64. We pointed out that the electoral system has completely transcended the American citizen, if the only choice is between two evils, or rather three this time around. We asked him how he can even term the system democratic if the people can't vote for someone they want for President. Not only that but we noted that men like Hitler have come to power with this kind of choice: "the lesser of two evils." He was left looking like an idiot. I am convinced that America must listen to the young people. All of us "teeny boppers" looked far more impressive than the oldsters and we were the only people who could come up with some real alternatives. Faith in the American way was the only line Salinger could come with. I hate to sound like a broken record but the people of Germany had faith in the German way too....

Despite his big cigar, Salinger did not impress us at that party rally. Terry jumped up on a grand piano and harangued him with some pointed questions about the war, then started chanting "Cleaver for President" (referring to black activist Eldridge Cleaver). Most of the young U.S. students joined in.

Later at a dance Terry and I spotted the daughter of U.S. Ambassador Sargent Shriver and another young woman who was apparently her friend, both great looking. I danced with one and Terry the other. The Secret Service types hulking around the dance floor looked like we were driving them nuts.

Young people have to be allowed their arrogance, I guess, and there was plenty of it around in the sixties. But we did have our points. And we had the political passion it takes to drive the points home. Anyway, my mother had sent me an article about AWOL soldiers and in that same letter dated October 6, I responded to it:

> About the article concerning AWOL soldiers; some of it is correct and some false. To begin with, when I came to France the army was denying the number of AWOLs I was eating supper with once a week. The article claims a Defense Department survey "revealed that over the past two years only 282 members of the armed forces went AWOL." There are more servicemen than that in Canada alone. Plus the fact the Army had recently admitted many AWOLs in Saigon and of course some AWOLs are fighting for the NLF. I think the way the Defense Department gets around the true figures is by classifying us as absentees while revealing AWOL figures. Last year they boasted that the desertion rate was down; however they failed to add no one was being classified as deserters. The number of airplanes shot down are counted in a similar way. We of RITA don't consider ourselves deserters. As the army would have a hard time proving it anyway. They must prove intent never to return to convict us. I carry my ID card with me at all times in case Charles [de Gaulle] changes his mind or the CIA gets ideas of getting me on the sly, which isn't entirely impossible....

I went on to tell my family for the first time, however vaguely, that I was planning to leave France: "At this time I don't think it wise to say where. It is not an eastern country; so don't worry about the 'dirty reds' getting ahold of me. I have been sufficiently 'brainwashed' anyway." There was a little of the old bitterness in that last remark.

About a week later, I wrote to my sister Nancy. It was a lengthy political harangue interspersed with snippets of my daily life, including my job at the appliance store, its owner, I wrote, "a member of the Communist Party, which is a major contradiction in itself, but the place is very easy to work in." Politics were never far from my mind.

I told Nancy that I wanted to visit a socialist country, especially Cuba. Some friends of mine had been there in August.

The tenth anniversary of Fidel Castro's triumph was at hand. I extolled the accomplishments of his revolution—the crushing of class inequality, radical advances in education, nutrition and health care, so that children were no longer malnourished and illiteracy was all but erased.

"It takes strong propaganda to reform people's thoughts from racism, individualism and opportunism," I wrote. "The Revolution must become a total thing or it won't work. It won't work because of the counterrevolutionaries always waiting to tear down men working for the common good of the people."

Unfortunately, it took more than "strong propaganda" to complete the Cuban revolution. I did not mention the suppression of civil liberties, or the execution or imprisonment of political enemies. But I still wonder what would have happened in Cuba if the United States had not imposed its embargo.

I ended that letter telling my sister, "If you are searching for Nancy Perrin you won't find her in half-truths or conformity, because that is not her. I know my sister and she wants the truth and nothing but the truth. You found it along with me in Chicago and you will find it again, but only if you are not afraid to." That reference to our summer in Chicago and the rally led by Martin Luther King is significant. Its impact upon both of us was surely deeper than we imagined at the time. All told, though, I sometimes wish I could be as sure about things today as I was in Paris in 1968.

On December 18, my mother wrote me a Christmas letter. There was the usual family stuff, but there were also some counterarguments to the material I had been sending home:

> We had a patient recently at the VA who had returned from a year at the Army installation near Kitzingen 30 days previously. He never heard of *Act*. He knew of some deserters but not by name. Of course I didn't tell him I was the mother of one....
>
> Many people ask about you and when and if you are returning to the USA. Especially lately we have inquiries on our Christmas cards. Even we would like to know if you are planning to ever return to this country and us. Your letters contain too much politics and too little of your personal life. It is quite impolite to try to force one's political beliefs on another, the same as it would be to do likewise with religion.

113

No doubt I wrote about politics because I wanted to justify my actions and have my parents understand (and maybe someday even approve of) what I had done. But I also wrote so much about politics because politics consumed so much of my personal life. There was no real distinction between the two and my mother was not hearing that. She ended her letter rather shrewdly: "I don't think the CIA or the Army wants you. You are no doubt giving them more information with your present activities than if they had you in confinement, at less expense."

In any case, by the time I got her letter I was well into my preparations to leave France. All I needed was a place to go. Sweden didn't interest me and neither did the eastern bloc countries. Cuba did interest me and I gave it serious consideration. I went to the Cuban embassy, which was upstairs over the American Express office by the Opera. I walked in and asked to speak to the ambassador, but was told he was in Havana and would I speak to one of his assistants. I showed the embassy official a collection of newspaper clippings about my activities, including my time with Stokely Carmichael, whom Havana seemed to trust. The official said that before they could allow me into Cuba they would have to investigate me to make sure I wasn't an American agent and the investigation could take months.

But I didn't feel that I had those months to spare. I wanted to get out of France. So I let the idea of Cuba drop, but I sometimes wish that I had gone there, at least for a while. At times it seemed that the only way I could sort out my politics was to go to a socialist country, see what life was like there, talk to people, find out for myself what was good and what was bad. Whatever the good intentions of those revolutions, an awful lot was bad and I knew it. But why?

It is curious how over the years whenever I had a chance to meet people from communist countries, or had conversations with Marxists in the West, I was critical of what was going on in those countries. And yet, when I talked with right-wing people, I would defend the communist countries. A common argument that I have heard from some leftists as long as I have been involved in politics is that the ultimate goal, and the ultimate good, is the establishment of socialism, when humans would finally achieve equality. That was the goal and whatever it took to achieve it was all right. For some time I accepted a good deal of that argument. But it seems that under the most promising of circumstances—Cuba and Nicaragua are both examples of this—equality doesn't happen. Now, I don't believe anything good can come out of violence or lying. I don't think the old ways of achieving substantial change will work anymore. I believe in electoral democracy, but some how or other we need to achieve economic democracy. All that aside, I needed to get out of France.

Through some friends I met a man from Tanzania, Nsa Kaisi, a reporter for the *Nationalist & Uhuru* in Dar as Salaam. He was involved with the Mozambique liberation movement called Frelimo. He proposed that I go there to maintain and drive an ambulance. My assignment would be to drive wounded liberation fighters from Mozambique to hospital in Tanzania.

I gave his proposal brief consideration but decided that, with my relatively dark complexion and dark hair, I looked a little too Portuguese and some righteous liberator might mistake me for his enemy. No, it was a little too adventuresome for me.

Then someone told me about an Icelandic Airlines pilot who would certainly be sympathetic. I met him at a sidewalk café near the Opera and asked him if he could perhaps disguise me as a flight crewman and smuggle me into New York from Amsterdam. I thought I could make my way to Canada from New York. He looked at me as if I were nuts and declined.

I was beginning to think my exile from the United States would be a long one, maybe even permanent. Canada appealed to me because culturally it was similar to the United States and the language in most of the country was English. Quebec was the major exception, of course, but I had learned enough French to get along there, too.

Ron told me he knew some people from San Diego who were teaching in the province of Saskatchewan, wherever that was. Some of my French friends told me there was a social-democratic government there. That sounded interesting.

So, during those last few weeks of 1968, I saved every franc I could get my hands on. Finally, in January of the new year, I sold almost everything I owned, which wasn't a hell of a lot—a small record player, the shortwave radio Ron had given me, records, books. That would have given me enough money to buy a one-way Air Canada ticket to Montreal. Then the French franc was devalued and I had to scrounge around for more money and that took another week or two. But, finally, around the middle of January, I boarded an Air Canada flight.

But when you are AWOL from your military unit in Germany, have no passport, have lived as an expatriate guest of the French government for a year and a half, boarding a plane to fly from Paris to Montreal is not necessarily a walk in the park. All I had was my military ID card and an expired California driver's license. My travel documents were inadequate, so I didn't want to give the airline people a good look at my credentials if I could help it. Max and Terry and I lurked around the boarding gate until the ground crew started pulling the stairs away from the jetliner (there were no all-weather gates then). Then I said a hasty goodbye, rushed up to the counter, flashed my papers and was allowed through. The woman checking papers yelled out the door and the stairs were pushed back to the plane. I bounded across the tarmac, up the stairs, and before entering the plane, turned and gave my friends a discreet clenched fist.

Home free? Not for a second. When I looked down the aisle, there facing me were a bunch of hefty, clean-cut, crew-cut guys who looked for all the world like a squad of FBI agents. They turned out to be a Canadian hockey team returning home, but I didn't know that as I edged past them with my heart punching at my rib cage.

I came to an empty third seat by a young couple. She was doing beadwork. His hair was long. It looked like a comfortable place to sit. So there I was, taking another leap into the unknown that would land me closer to home but still in exile. The possibilities stretched west across the ocean, vast and sometimes as foreboding as the Canadian prairie that awaited me.

THE EARLY CANADA YEARS

Apprehension, a lot of it, was what I remember feeling on that flight from Paris to Montreal. I had no idea what I would find, but it would probably be less dangerous than driving an ambulance in Mozambique, so that was some consolation.

The people I sat with during the flight turned out to be a Jewish couple returning from Israel. We talked a lot and became quite friendly. They were from New York City. I was relieved when he confided that he was a draft dodger, that they were headed for Canada because they were concerned he would be drafted into the Israeli army. They knew something of the world, about exile and a choice of countries, and I felt I could trust them. Before we landed I gave them the telephone number of a civil rights lawyer in New York and asked them to call him if immigration officials arrested me at the airport.

As it turned out, there were no problems. It was taking a risk to trust people I'd known for only a few hours on an airplane, but the customs agent asked me only a few simple questions and passed me on through. I was afraid to acknowledge the Jewish couple behind me, so I walked straight out of there and never looked back.

The bus ride from the airport to downtown Montreal gave me my first look at Canada. I remember thinking it didn't look an awful lot different than the United States—same housing, convenience stores on the corner, shopping malls. But it still amazes me that a young man who grew up about a hundred miles south of the Canadian border could have known so little about that

117

country. In those days, the salient image I had of Canada was from an old TV series about Sergeant Preston of the Yukon, and for all I know that was filmed somewhere else.

After I got off the bus at the Queen Elizabeth hotel, I caught a cab to the address of my old friend from Paris, Phil Wagner. Phil was a bit older than the rest of us. He had a college degree and had been involved in the Peace Corps before he was drafted. I remembered him talking about working in South America, somewhere on the west coast, maybe in Chile. He was tall, quiet, well spoken. He had worked with Terry and me and a few others on our newsletter *Act*. Socially he found his own friends outside our group so I didn't spend a lot of time with him. He left France a few months before I did and we kept in touch. You'll remember I took Philip's job at FNAC.

A little bald-headed guy opened the door. He was wearing robes. There were lots of candles burning and a statue of Buddha at the far end of the room. Somewhere along the line Phil had become a Buddhist and I had walked into a small temple in Montreal. The man told me I could find Phil across the street. Phil said I could stay with him until I made arrangements to head west to Saskatchewan.

Some of Ron's friends who had studied with him under Marcuse were teaching at the University of Saskatchewan, Regina Campus, and they'd said they would help me if I could make my way there. Before I got to Canada and looked at a map I had no idea where Saskatchewan was in relation to other provinces. I didn't even know how to pronounce the name.

While I was making plans to leave France and go to Canada, my friend Terry Klug was making plans to turn himself in and return to the United States. And that is what he did. Terry wanted to talk with American soldiers about the war and he was willing to go to jail to make that happen. The day after I left Paris, U.S. authorities flew Terry back to the States. He ended up in the stockade at Fort Dix, New Jersey, where he got involved in a prisoner riot. Some of the rioters came to be called the Fort Dix 38 and got long sentences, twenty or thirty years, for being involved in the riot, but Terry was acquitted on the riot charges. Probably the publicity he got for turning himself in helped. But he was court-martialed for desertion and sentenced to three years in the federal prison at Leavenworth.

It may be that we both got out of France just in time. The French government's attitude toward foreigners involved in leftist political activity had changed since the Events of May. The heat was on. The police summoned Max and handed him a deportation order shortly after Terry and I left. He appealed, but it must have been clear to him things were winding down.

Max Cook was really Tomi Schweitzer. He grew up in Vienna. His father was a doctor and his mother a psychologist (some reports say they were both psychoanalysts, in the tradition of Freud, no doubt). They were Jews and fled Vienna for France in 1938.

Max's father could not find work in France, so he took his ten-year-old son with him to London and left his wife in Paris. According to James Reston Jr. in his book *The Amnesty of John David Herndon* (New York: McGraw-Hill, 1973), Max's father could not find work in London, either, and eventually killed himself. (Some of the biographical details come from Reston's book, other's from what Max told me himself.)

Max told me that he had become politicized as a boy in London. It seems he had a pet rabbit caged in the back yard and a German rocket blast killed it. He said he joined the Young Communist League to fight the bastards who killed his rabbit. Probably there is a certain tallness to that tale, but it is typical Max.

What probably affected Max far more deeply was the death of his grandmother and an uncle at the hands of the Nazis, to say nothing of the loss of his father, who can only be counted as another victim of fascism. In any case, Max launched himself early into what became a lifetime of left-wing activism.

His mother managed to escape Vichy France to Spain on a false Mexican visa. She was reunited with Max in New York. That was in 1944, according to Reston. In the United States, Max went on to study geophysics while keeping up his political activities. (I will keep calling him Max because that's the name I knew and still know him by. Although his wife Simone called him Tomi.)

Max told me he fled the United States in the 1950s because agents of Senator Joseph McCarthy's communist witch-hunt were hounding him. (I don't think I'd ever heard of the "McCarthy era" or the House Un-American Activities Committee (HUAC) before meeting Max. Was I not paying attention or did they fail to teach it in American history class?) Reston says Max fled to France to evade the draft during the Korean War (Max actually went first to Israel, not France).

Max talked a lot about the persecution of communists. He took me to the building in Paris where Lenin lived, having been exiled by the czar. At the Père Lachaise cemetery, he showed me the wall against which the leaders of the Paris Commune were shot in 1871.

Max told me he eventually landed a job with a French oil company. Using that employment as a cover, he was able to move in and out of Algeria and help revolutionaries there in their war against the French colonists (1954-1962).

Later, Max went to Cuba to help with the Castro government's search for oil. He claimed that Fidel stole his girlfriend. But I think Max would have been quite at ease with sacrificing his love interest to "the revolution."

After dining at Max and Simone's bookstore one evening, Max got out his slides and projector. I was astonished to see shots of Fidel playing baseball with his brother Raul. Max said Raul was the better player.

As I said earlier, shortly after I left France Max was summoned to the prefecture and handed a deportation order. He appealed and in March signed a vague statement that he would not engage in any political activity, a statement that I doubt he took at all seriously.

Then, in June, he was buying a newspaper on the boulevard Saint-Germain when four government toughs grabbed him, shouting that he was wanted for armed robbery. Seeing people watch from a nearby café, Max yelled that he was being kidnapped, that it was another Dreyfus affair. No one responded. A gendarme approached but backed off when he realized the abductors were cops.

They took Max to the Ministry of the Interior where he was interrogated and then jailed. Later, after an unsuccessful attempt to deport him to Austria (involving an airport fiasco during which the Austrian pilot refused to let him board because he did not have an Austrian passport), they flew him to Corsica, where he spent several months under house arrest. In October, agents snatched him again and this time deported him to Austria.

French opposition leader Francois Mitterand, who later became president of France, asked Minister of the Interior Ramon Marcellin about Max's deportation. It took Marcellin nearly a year to reply.

Meanwhile, Max returned to Paris surreptitiously in February 1970 to take his doctoral exams at the Sorbonne. Of course he was in the country illegally and was soon picked up and deported back to Austria. That generated a scandal at the university and the government agreed to allow Max back into France on a weekend visa so he could take his exams. Max heard about it on the radio in Heidelberg. He returned to Paris, passed the exams, and was tailed all the way back to Germany.

Finally, in September of that year, Marcellin responded before the National Assembly to Mitterand's query about Max. According to Reston, he called Max "a notorious rabble-rouser, and foreigner, part Lenin and part James Bond, an organizer of Maoist students, who even wore a Mao jacket to his doctoral exams. My guess is that Max enjoyed that description immensely and had a good laugh about the James Bond part.

Later, Reston reports, Simone wrote to someone high in the French legal system and Max's expulsion was quashed in July 1971. Apparently Max and Simone had even more connections than I knew about.

Max was an interesting character, all right, and I liked him. But he was a zealot and zealots, whether political or religious, make me uneasy because they all seem to use any method necessary to achieve their goals. At the very least truth and reality get stretched.

****

A day or two after arriving in Montreal, I phoned home. Mom answered. She was surprised to hear my voice, even more surprised that I was in Montreal, less than two hundred miles from Springfield. I said I was eager to see them all and asked if they would come to Montreal. By then my sister Nancy was away at college in Massachusetts, but my brother David was still at home.

I told Mom I would call back that evening after Dad got back from the barbershop. I asked her not to tell him that I was going to call because I wanted to surprise him and speak to him in French. He was born in France in 1909 and spoke French fluently. His family emigrated to Quebec when he was a boy and a few years later they moved to Vermont. So the family had a strong French tradition and I thought Dad would be pleased to have one of his boys call home and speak to him in French. As we have seen, he hadn't been pleased with a lot that I had done in the past couple of years, so I guess I was looking for anything that might meet with his approval.

I knew what time he would be coming in from the barbershop. When I was a boy, I used to go and help him sweep up after he closed at six. Then we would go back to the house and I would sometimes get his jug of wine out from under the kitchen counter. He always kept a gallon jug of wine there and liked to sip a glass or two to unwind.

So that evening I called Dad and spoke to him in French, although we soon retreated into English. He said they would come to Montreal. The next weekend Dad, Mom and David drove up and I stayed with them at their motel for a couple of days. It was a joy to see them. David, tall and blond, a basketball player, had grown a lot in the year and a half since I had last seen him. He was about fifteen. I remember arm wrestling with him at the motel. There is a photograph of us sitting on a couch. Mom and David have their arms around each others shoulders. I am sitting apart. Mom and Dave were always close.

Overall that visit went well. We talked for hours, some of it about politics. They did not try to convince me to turn myself in and we ended up on good terms. I was surprised to find that both Mom and Dad were beginning to understand what the antiwar movement was all about, what the peace movement was all about, although not completely by any means.

We watched Nixon's inaugural address on the motel TV. When Nixon had finished, Dad said, "There, what's wrong with that?"

"Nothing," I said. Nixon had spoken of peace and prosperity and who could argue with that? The war did not end, however.

The following weekend my sister Nancy came up from Massachusetts. She took me to the Expo site, where she had been in 1967 for the world fair. She was a high school junior that year, the year I went AWOL, and she said later she saw me as distant and uncommunicative and she didn't understand what I was doing. That was a hard time for her because a lot of people saw the whole family as subversive. She was angry with me. But she used money our parents had given her for college to fly to Montreal to see me that weekend. Mom was not happy about that. But the next year she did it again. She flew to New York City to meet with some of the people I was with at Fort Sill in the hope that she would understand me better. She became more of an activist. In a recollection I asked her to write in 1991, she said, "I think that the gift we have received from my brother is to look beyond what meets the eye."

After those two weekends, I had the feeling that the rift between my family and me was mending at last.

I was eager to get on to Saskatchewan, but I came down with the flu and that kept me in Montreal two weeks longer than I had intended. The extra time, though, enabled Maryann Weissman, the Youth Against War and Fascism woman who did time for attempting to attend the Fort Sill courts-martial, to come up from New York and visit for a few hours. It was good to see her especially when she handed me a hundred dollars. I lived off it for quite a while.

Finally, the second week of February I boarded a bus to Saskatchewan. It was a forty-eight hour trip. What I remember most is that as we headed west the air kept getting colder and colder. Much of the scenery was beautiful, particularly around Lake Superior. As we rounded the lake and passed through Thunder Bay (then two towns as I recall, Fort William and Port Arthur) and headed toward Dryden and Kenora, I liked what I saw. I always liked the outdoors, hunting and fishing, and just being there. That country seemed made for it and reminded me how much I missed Vermont.

Apart from that, it was fun watching people get on and off the bus. When we stopped for coffee breaks, I overheard conversations and wondered about Canada and Canadians. Every time we stopped for a break, one guy pumped coins into the jukebox. It drove me nuts because he always played the same tune, "Little Arrows." No doubt the song had some bearing on his life, but I didn't care if I ever heard it again. For better or worse, that is the way the world seems to work, on issues big and small.

Not long after our rest stop in Kenora, Ontario, I settled back into my seat and dozed off for a couple of hours. When I woke up, I looked out the window and what I saw was downright alarming. We were in Manitoba. This was prairie. The forest, lakes and streams were behind now. And I had never seen such a desolate-looking place in my life. All I could see was blowing snow, snow blowing across the highway, snow blowing everywhere, on what must have been the flattest land on earth. It was everything I had imagined Siberia to be. Maybe there was more than one way for a government to send dissenters to Siberia.

The trip around Lake Superior had been cold, but now the bus windows were frosting up. As we pulled into Winnipeg, the driver announced that the temperature was thirty degrees below zero. Southern Vermont never gets that cold. There were a lot of religious and political signs around the city. One read, "Wayward youth, Jesus is the way." I thought, "Oh, my God, I haven't seen a sign like that since the South. Where am I going?" There were also advertisements for the NDP. I didn't know what NDP stood for (New Democratic Party), much less that I would eventually be employed by it.

On the last leg of the trip, from Winnipeg to Regina, the scenery didn't change at all. It seemed that my heart was sinking with the temperature. What kind of godforsaken place had I condemned myself to? By the time we hit Regina, the mercury had plunged to forty degrees below zero. It was about ten o'clock at night. Few people were out in the bitter cold and there was an eerie feeling in the nearly deserted streets. An occasional car would leave billowing clouds of exhaust steam. Ice crystals danced under streetlights, swirling behind any moving vehicle.

As we swung into the bus terminal on Hamilton Street, the tires didn't squeak on the snow the way they do on the coldest nights in Vermont; here they screeched in agony, as if to say it was too damn cold. When the bus door opened, a cloud of steam boiled into the night air. I stepped down through the cloud onto the snow and ice and drew my first breath of Saskatchewan air. It hurt. My lungs seemed to yowl in protest. I learned quickly that at forty below you don't take deep breaths. Frozen lungs don't work well.

Before I left Paris, some of my acquaintances had told me Saskatchewan had some interesting politics. North America's first socialist government had been elected there in 1944. Government intervention in the economy had been extensive and North America's first experiment in socialized medicine was instituted in 1961. But it didn't feel all that interesting in the cold-crunched February night at the bus station in Regina. And even less interesting when I learned that social democrats were no longer governing.

Ron had given me the names of three people who had studied with him in San Diego and were now teaching in Regina: Jim Bauerlein, Lowell Bergman and Bill Leiss. They were expecting me sometime that winter. I phoned Bill from the bus station and he said he would be down to pick me up. He showed up with his wife Judy and as we were leaving the station they turned and looked me over and said they would have to do something about winter clothing.

I haven't seen or heard much of Bill for more than twenty-five years, but for the first couple of years I lived in Canada he was vital for me, both emotionally and financially. In many ways, he was almost a parent to me and he is one of the finest people I have ever met.

Like Ron, Bill had studied philosophy with Marcuse and he later published some of his own work. He was a studious guy. Tall, slim, with a chiseled face, he was always looking off into space as if he were deep in thought. His philosophy was radical but his lifestyle was quite conservative. The only music he liked was classical, although he did try Bob Dylan and the Moody Blues. Last I heard he was a department head at Simon Fraser University in Vancouver.

Judy had a wild streak about her and was frustrated. They were a mismatch and they separated not long after I got there. Bill bought her things in an attempt to appease her. She threatened to have affairs. That left me feeling uncomfortable, because we would be sitting around the living room and she would, in very graphic language, talk of stepping out. Bill would sit there and act as if he didn't care whether she did or not.

For the first two months in Saskatchewan, I lived with Bill and Judy. They bought me winter clothing and took me with them

to their social engagements. Bill was a marvelous cook and he saw
to it that I didn't undergo some kind of culinary shock by moving
from Paris to Regina.

One of the fonder memories I have of those two months
centers around a young woman who spent quite a lot of time at the
house. She was warm, kind and concerned. Our involvement was
brief but intense—an intimacy that, for my part at least, was long
overdue. It had been two years since I'd seen Cyndy in California
and during my seventeen months in Paris I had been intimate with
only one woman, a leftist student from Tours named Fabienne.
Apart from that involvement which lasted only a few weeks, most
of my interest and energy went into politics.

About ten years ago, I happened to run into that woman I
was with in Regina. She had matured into a person with an almost
regal presence about her.

Although I had been in Paris less than two years, a lot had
changed in North America. Braless young women were open in
their flirtations, nothing coy about it. And the music! Virtually all
the American music played in Paris was either jazz or R&B. The
people I met in Regina were listening to music with screeching
guitars and incomprehensible lyrics and I didn't like it.

During those first weeks in Regina, I hung out mainly on
the University of Saskatchewan campus, where I attended political
meetings and sat in on some classes. Once I sat in the front row of
a lecture hall listening to Quebec separatist René Lévesque talk. At
one point his eyes widened and his voice stumbled. I turned behind
me to the left to see what had distracted him. There sat a woman
pulling her baby to her large, swollen and very exposed breasts.

Generally I kept a low profile because I didn't have any
official status to be in the country. The Canadian government had a
policy of granting landed immigrant status to American draft
dodgers, but had said nothing about deserters.

Finally, the government announced in March that deserters
from the United States armed forces could apply for immigration
and be treated like any other applicant. At the same time, although
I wasn't aware of it, another of Ron's friends there, Lowell
Bergman, was investigating the likelihood of my success with the
immigration point system. Applicants were assessed mostly by
their financial resources, education and employment potential.

Lowell determined that acceptance was possible but not a sure thing and he knew I couldn't afford the consequences of an unsuccessful application.

Of all those I met who had studied with Ron in San Diego, Lowell was the wildest. He liked to take personal risks, such as getting involved with a Regina motorcycle gang and trying to radicalize them politically. The gang members had the biker trappings—cutoff sleeves, tattoos. But they didn't have motorcycles.

Lowell was of medium height and build with unruly hair. He looked like the quintessential SDS radical. He was always trying to find the limit, if only by pushing the university administration. Some claimed that he got Eldridge Cleaver from the U.S., through Canada and into Cuba. In any case, he went back to the States in that summer of 1969 and years later became a producer for "60 Minutes." For about fourteen years he worked with Mike Wallace on that show—until CBS backed away from a story he had produced based on a tobacco company whistle-blower, former Brown & Williamson executive Jeffrey Wigand.

Angered by CBS's cowardice, Lowell ended up consulting on a movie about the affair. After seeing the movie script, Wallace felt that Lowell had betrayed him although Lowell said he did not write the script and had little control over it. But Lowell's time with "60 Minutes" was over and he went on to produce network news stories for other shows. The movie, *The Insider*, was released late in 1999. Al Pacino played Lowell.

One evening back in April 1969, Lowell invited me to a party on Albert Street near downtown Regina. Three young women were renting the apartment and there were a lot of people there when I arrived. Most of them I hadn't met. For a while I sipped beer and engaged in small talk around the room. Later I moved over to a window and gazed down on Albert Street. It was still cold and there wasn't much traffic but for some reason I was feeling contemplative.

Suddenly, I felt a hand on my shoulder. I turned and saw an attractive woman gazing back at me. She was tall and slim, with reddish-blond hair. She smiled and said, "Hi. My name is Karen. I understand that we're going to get married and I think we ought to talk about it." That was shocking!

Later I learned that Lowell had approached a group of women active in the local New Left movement and asked if one of them would marry me to remove the risk from my immigration application. After some discussion, Jill Anweiller volunteered, but her boyfriend, Gord Kennard, balked at the idea. Karen was the second volunteer to step forward, but she wanted to meet me before she committed herself. That was why I was invited to the party. Karen was one of the three women renting the apartment.

After the others had gone and her roommates were in bed, Karen and I sat on the living room couch and talked for hours. We ended up making love on that couch and a month later Karen Howe and I were married. We were together for the next seven years. What had been planned as a "political union" turned out to be the real thing. Or at least it seemed that way at first.

After a honeymoon in Banff, Alberta, amid a magnificent mountain landscape, I applied for landed immigrant status and then came the long wait for a decision. Meanwhile I was in limbo and legally I couldn't take a job. So we rented an inexpensive farmhouse at the intersection of highways 10 and 210, near the resort area of the Qu'Appelle Valley. That summer we had a great time. Guests from the city streamed in and we partied for three months.

The lung-searing cold was gone, of course, and I had learned that it was indeed possible for human beings to live in that kind of extreme climate. But there was another aspect of that prairie that scared me at first. It was the vulnerability I felt from having nothing around me—no trees, no hills—the feeling of being totally exposed to nature's will. I started adjusting to it by doing a lot of exploring, driving all over the place in a beat-up Volkswagen van I bought and fixed. I discovered that there is a lot of life on that land if you take the time to look for it. Lots of wildlife, much more than in Vermont. Years later, I took Dad hunting in Saskatchewan and we each bagged our limit in three species of game birds. But that was hard to believe when I first arrived and couldn't understand how anything could live there.

I remember one night that summer when Karen, Lowell Bergman and I went for a walk. It never really gets dark there in summer. The northern sky is light all night long. The sun comes up in the northeast, almost in the north. Late in the evening it sets in the northwest, then through the night you can watch its light move across the northern horizon until it rises again about four in the morning. It was late when we went walking. We stood out there, a long way from any tree or building and suddenly I got this feeling like we were on a disk in space. There was no variation at all on the horizon as you turned 360 degrees. The three of us stood out there in the middle of the prairie and it was the first time I experienced the sensation of the earth hurtling through space. Is there any place on earth, no matter how forbidding, that does not have an awesome beauty uniquely its own?

Another person who showed up that summer was my high school classmate Tim Closson. He is the guy who drove me from Poway to the airport in LA when I was on my way to Fort Sill. I was sitting in the bathtub and heard Karen greet someone at the door downstairs. Moments later the bathroom door opened and there stood Tim. He was tall, slim, with chiseled features and sad eyes. (He lives in Idaho now and at fifty-plus years can look remarkably like Abraham Lincoln.) My first thought was that the U.S. government had sent him. That—and my nakedness in the bathtub—made for an awkward hello.

Tim went back downstairs and I finished my bath. Then I went down and met his wife Debbie and his son Sean. By then I was convinced that Tim was an agent and I thought my suspicion was confirmed when he told me he had been in the Army and was AWOL. He had never been a political type. In high school, he was my hot rod buddy. Another classmate, Russ Shaw, had been the friend who had interest in social matters. Russ and I listened to the Beatles, Bob Dylan and the We Five. Tim and I listened to the Beach Boys. It didn't make sense to me then that Tim would be the one to show up in Canada.

Tim stayed in Regina for about two years, until Debbie left him and returned to her parents' home in northern Idaho. My relationship with Tim was cordial but distant. He never attempted to get involved in my politics and, as it turned out, he was not an agent after all.

Not long after Debbie left, Tim rejoined her in Idaho, living and working underground. Later his father died back in Vermont. Tim went to the funeral, after making arrangements with the FBI to turn himself in as soon as the service was over. If I remember right, they let him off with an undesirable discharge. He still lives in Idaho with his new wife Pat. I used to visit them but found after awhile we had little in common beyond an affection for old cars and trucks.

When September arrived with still no word from immigration and the winter not far off, Karen and I decided to move back into Regina. The influx of exiles from the States was increasing and finding places for them to stay was problematic, so Karen and I approached the local committee to aid U.S. war resisters, headed by Professor Dallas Smythe. They had been dealing with the new arrivals and we suggested that if they would raise the funds we would rent a house and provide shelter and immigration counseling. That was how we formed the Regina Committee of American Deserters. Smythe's committee helped us integrate into Canada over one hundred men, one AWOL woman and sometimes their families. All in one year.

We soon had three houses rented. Looking after the draft dodgers and deserters who were pouring in and maintaining the houses was a full-time job for both of us. The Canadian Council of Churches contributed a monthly stipend of two hundred dollars that provided for our personal needs.

One day that fall an officer from the Royal Canadian Mounted Police passport and immigration department came to the door. He asked me to come out to his car. I was shitting bricks as I sat on the front seat of that police car, door open, one foot on the ground in case I had to bolt for freedom.

The Mountie opened a dossier containing information on me supplied by the U.S. government, including documentation from my Army service records. The file must have been two inches thick. Then he pulled out copies of *Act* and asked if I was familiar with the publication. He asked if I knew or had ever known Stokely Carmichael. On and on he went, asking question after question. Finally, he simply smiled, thanked me and drove away. A short while later, to my surprise, I got my papers to stay in Canada.

The Regina police kept a watch on our three houses. Often an unmarked police car would park across the street for hours on end. Cops would follow me on foot about the city, too. After a while, I recognized their ghost cars, so I could keep an eye out for them. It wasn't hard because their license plates were in numerical order.

Partly because of that surveillance, our rules were strict: clean premises and absolutely no drugs allowed. And I told the residents that if they wanted to mess around with girls they should do it elsewhere. That was because one guy brought a girl around who looked like she might still be in high school.

Some of the exiles who stayed with us were Vietnam vets and they were pretty messed up. We did a lot of immigration counseling of course and sometimes had to get them psychiatric help. There was one vet who slept with a knife at hand and one night pulled it on an unsuspecting roommate. Then there was the guy I found sitting in a drugged stupor on the living room floor of house number three. The other guys said they didn't know what he had taken. I had to do something for him. Apart from that, if the guy died of an overdose or something it could have meant trouble for our organization. So I carried him out to the VW van and drove him to the emergency room. They pumped his stomach and kept him overnight for observation.

Another evening Karen and I were making our usual rounds and at that same house we were chatting with the guys. Karen was in the kitchen and I was in the living room. I heard a knock at the back door and then Karen greeting a new arrival. As I sat talking, I kept one ear on Karen's conversation. When I heard the new guy was from Vermont I excused myself and went into the kitchen. I asked him where in Vermont he was from. He said Rutland. My family had moved to Rutland from Holden, Massachusetts when I was five and we lived there until I was nine.

"Where in Rutland?"

"Killington Avenue." He told me the number, but that didn't help. I asked him if it was anywhere near the corner of Butterfly Avenue.

"Right on the corner."

"Not in the two-story gray house?"

"Yes."

It was the same house my family had lived in. My parents sold it to his parents when we moved away. He even had the same bedroom I had. He was nine when he moved in; I was nine when we moved out. He took up friendships with the kids in the neighborhood and graduated from high school with them. It was like hearing what would have been for me had we not moved away. A girl I went with to the movies (my first date, sort of) turned out to be the first girl he made love with. His family name is Noble and I have long since lost track of him, but in the late eighties I heard he was living in Ottawa, Ontario.

Some of our residents were draft dodgers, but most were deserters. The draft dodgers tended to be better educated. Many of the deserters hadn't graduated from high school. That made it hard for them to get immigration status. You did acquire extra points if you had a job offer, but only when applying at the border, so that played a part in one of our schemes. Let's just say we had to be innovative in circumventing some really nonsensical regulations.

A couple of guys who helped me with moving people around were Ray Kennedy and Barry Lipton. Together we had a great deal of success in getting papers for people, in some cases after they had been turned down elsewhere in Canada. Ray and I have remained close friends ever since.

Another new arrival at our house caught my attention because he was so neatly dressed and looked much "straighter" than most of the others. I think his first name was Scott, but remember well that his family name was Udall. I asked him if he was related to Stuart Udall, who was U.S. Secretary of the Interior in Kennedy's cabinet. He said, "Yeah, he's my Dad." I nearly fell off my chair.

I liked him. We had some good conversations. Stuart Udall came to Regina to see his son, but I missed meeting him as I was away in Vancouver on "business." He was a friend of Otto Lang, a Saskatchewan member of parliament and a cabinet minister in Pierre Trudeau's government and I believe they met at the time. Scott didn't stay around long and I don't remember where he went.

Don Frombach, a likeable guy from the Seattle area was one of the resisters I enjoyed having around. His stay was short; he ended up back in Washington. We had a few phone conversations after he left but I soon lost track of him.

The very first guy that Karen and I helped was Art Davis (of course not the Art Davis from Springfield). Art came and went for quite a while. I think he was from the Midwest somewhere.

One of the many people who helped us in those times was Bill Livant, a professor at the Regina campus of the University of Saskatchewan, now called the University of Regina. Bill hired me as a teaching assistant in his first year psychology course. A mere high school graduate, I headed my own seminar with about fifteen students, graded papers and prepared minilectures explaining the righteous cause of the world's oppressed. Several years later I met one of those students in Bartleby's, a downtown Regina bar. She told me it had been an interesting seminar.

Other Regina faculty members who helped us were Gerry Sperling, Milnor Alexander and Bob Sass. Gerry gave us financial support and encouraged me not only in the early Regina days but also over the years since. His first wife, Linda, coached Karen and me in the Lamaze birthing method. His current wife is Maggie Siggens, a well-known Canadian writer.

Milnor has been active her whole life, in the fifties combating the excesses of Joseph McCarthy, and she is still involved in progressive causes in Victoria, British Columbia.

Bob Sass was active in the Saskatchewan labor movement. Originally from New York City, he was a strong supporter.

Bill Gilbey, with the Saskatchewan Federation of Labour (Canadian readers will be pleased to note that I can still spell), had good contacts in Ottawa. We got several guys their papers with Bill's help.

Another one of the exiles who stands out in my memory is Billy Parrott, a tall, slender twenty-two-year-old soldier from Lloydville, Kentucky. Right from the time of his arrival, Billy was overenthusiastic. He wanted to be part of everything, although to me it was more like he wanted to stick his nose into everything. Early in 1970, he told *New York Times* correspondent Edward Cowan that he had been laid off from his job when the company found out he was a deserter. Cowan reported that American draft dodgers and deserters in the Regina area had trouble finding work and that was certainly true. The article said that estimates of the number of American antiwar refugees in Canada ranged from twenty thousand to sixty thousand, probably three to six thousand of them deserters. The U.S. Department of Defense claimed there were only five hundred seventy-six deserters in Canada.

One day Billy received a letter from a Marine sergeant stationed at Camp Lejeune, North Carolina. The letter threatened his life. Believing that one of the best ways to protect ourselves from that kind of harassment was to inform the Canadian public, I issued a press release about the letter. I also informed Tommy Douglas, former Saskatchewan premier and federal leader of the New Democratic Party. He had taken an interest in our work and had helped directly with our more difficult immigration cases. Unlike so many other elected politicians who have assistants running interference, Tommy always spoke with me directly from his office at the House of Commons. That kind of relationship with the leader of a national party offered us additional protection.

Several days later, out of breath with excitement, Billy showed up at the main house where Karen and I lived. He said he had seen the Marine sergeant in town, in a car with several other men.

Having previously discussed the threatening letter with the local police, I called them and told them that the sergeant had been spotted, gave them a description of the car as Billy had reported it, and informed them that we intended to defend ourselves.

Karen hurried out to collect firearms from friends around town. She came back with several rifles, shotguns and a lot of ammunition. Some of the guys in the house weren't too stable and I didn't want them handling loaded guns, so I laid all the weapons on the bed in the front bedroom, close by the front entrance in case we were attacked.

Several hours later a police officer came to the door. I again described what had happened and showed him the weapons on the bed. I also told him that the guys sitting around were all combat trained and some had battlefield experience and that we meant business. As he was leaving, he pointed to a poster on the living room wall and asked if I was the guy in the picture. I said, "No, that's Che Guevara." I'm not sure how he took all of that, but the police kept their distance and we were not attacked. After a few days, things returned to what passed as normal at the time.

Several weeks later, Billy disappeared and we didn't hear from him for months. Then he called me late one night, said he was in Colorado and had been arrested and the Weathermen had broken him out. He wanted my help. But that was a bit much. I'd had enough of Billy Parrott and his stories. I have no idea what he was up to, but I shudder now to recall how that episode in Regina could have put us in way over our heads.

Our work went on. The second house we used was right next door to ours, both on 1300 block Hamilton Street. One evening the guys living there came over to get me. They said someone new had just arrived. We went over and talked to him and I noticed right away that his arms were a little short for his stature. His answers to a few questions were enough to convince me that he had never been in the military, so I told him that his claim to be a deserter was phony. He confessed that he had escaped from a state mental hospital in Illinois and was afraid to go back because they would give him shock treatment. Wouldn't you know that I had just finished reading *One Flew Over the Cuckoo's Nest.* Maybe the new arrival had, too.

So I called a man I knew through the Mennonite minister, Fred Unruh. Fred and many of his parishioners were a great help to us in those days. The man I contacted was a senior official in the provincial department of social services and he promised to hold what I had to say in confidence. I didn't want to send anyone to shock treatment so I asked that the story be checked out with Illinois authorities to find out if the guy was dangerous or anything.

My contact, Otto Driedger, checked it out and the story was true. Our guy had escaped and was not dangerous. He was mildly retarded and his mother had committed him when he was twelve years old, claiming that he was too difficult to handle.

Otto kept his word and let me deal with the situation. I found the guy a kitchen job at a resort camp, a retreat kind of place, in British Columbia. Meanwhile he had proved to be resourceful on his own. The circus was in town and he found a temporary job helping out with the elephants, shoveling dung, which, when you think about it, must have been a considerable amount of work.

Later he changed his mind and said he missed his friends at the institution. We turned him over to the Canadian authorities and they sent him back. Karen and I were sad to see him go. He was a very likeable guy.

135

That story illustrates how important it was for us to maintain our independence. Many of the political groups wanted us to align with them. But we worked with anyone who agreed to help us—Liberals, Trotskyites, Quakers, Mennonites, whoever.

Also in 1970, as I recall, a Regina service club sponsored a concert by the U.S. Army Band at a Regina High School. Several dozen demonstrators showed up and Karen and I were among them. As the concert began in the school auditorium, we all tried to force our way in, yelling and chanting. There was a scuffle. Margo Bauerlein was the only one who managed to get through the melee into the concert and make her way to the stage. Not knowing how else to express herself, she pulled off her jersey and exposed her bare breasts to the audience.

Karen and one or two others were arrested. The leaders of all Regina's left-wing organizations were charged, including one who was in Mexico that day. The charges were minor, disorderly conduct or the like, but they were not minor for me because I was not a citizen and I could have been deported if convicted.

Lawyer Jim Crane, a really good guy, represented us. He was small and appeared to be meek, but he surprised me when he turned out to be an effective spark plug in the courtroom. The prosecution had no particular evidence against any individual, so all the charges were dismissed.

That summer of 1970 I traveled with another Vietnam War resister and a Canadian guy to an American exiles conference in Montreal. We rode in my old humpbacked style Volvo, which by then had replaced the VW van, and camped out along the way. The first night we stopped after dark and slept under the stars. At daybreak, we found ourselves in a farmer's front yard. We spent the second night in a tent on the north shore of Lake Superior. We swam in the lake and cooked on an open fire. The third night we slept in an apple orchard northwest of Ottawa. During the conference, we stayed in a roach-ridden apartment in downtown Montreal.

I don't remember much about the conference except that Tom Hayden was guest speaker. He said that if there wasn't a revolution in the United States within a few years the world was doomed. Tom, of course, later married Jane Fonda. Mom and Dad came up for a short visit.

After the conference I was scheduled to meet with some people doing aid and counseling to draft dodgers and deserters in Toronto. Heading toward Toronto, we got as far as Kingston and were suddenly hit with homesickness. At least I remember missing Karen. We decided to head northwest and drive straight through to Regina, spelling each other at the wheel. Not too far west of Wawa, I woke up from my turn to sleep in the back seat and saw that we were speeding along on the wrong side of the road. The driver's chin was on his chest. I didn't say anything, just reached forward and turned the wheel to the right. That woke him up. And I drove the rest of the way.

By the fall of 1970 I was growing weary of the intense life we were leading. Three years of living pretty much on the lam, keeping half a step in front of the authorities, had taken their toll. And I didn't like what those years had done to me. Mistrustful and quick tempered, I was angry a lot of the time and Karen was usually the one I unloaded on. As I mentioned before, I now see that anger was the way I expressed my hurt and fear. Our marriage had been shaky ever since our honeymoon trip to Banff. We knew each other only a month and until we had had that time alone together we didn't discuss what kind of relationship we should try to build in our marriage. I was risking all that I could through the political work and was looking for a relatively traditional marriage. At Banff, I discovered that Karen wanted a more open, experimental model. Her words and behavior from that time on rocked me, put me continually on the defensive, tipped me back onto my heels as it were. And that was not my favorite position. The political work had made me proactive even aggressive at times, but with Karen I was more reactive as I struggled to meet her on her ground. That effort made me feel hurt and fearful a lot of the time and when I felt really boxed in, cornered, I lashed out in a rage. I think if Karen and I had courted under more normal circumstances we would have realized that we were not a suitable match as long-term partners.

Obviously, I am talking about this now with 20/20 hindsight. At the time, I didn't have a clue. What the hell were we fighting about? Now I readily admit that I simply could not handle having been through the struggle of the Vietnam dilemma only to find myself involved with a woman who wanted to tear down the traditional notions of marriage. The Vietnam experience was enough to deal with and I was trying to keep a lid on the "new" stuff. Karen was trying to pry the lid off.

I did love Karen. But, in my hunger for a more normal lifestyle, I thought that if we settled into the mainstream maybe our marriage would mellow. So I arranged for another exile couple to take over the operation of our organization. Apart from my relationship with Karen, that ended three years of looking over my shoulder, never sitting in a public place if I couldn't see who was coming and going, always keeping my eyes open for an alternative exit. I wasn't brought up to live that way. Three years was enough, although I'm proud I did my part to oppose that dirty stinking war.

Karen and I took jobs at a residential treatment center for severely emotionally disturbed children. That didn't turn out to be the place to get away from intensity—not by a long shot—and we worked there for only a few months.

Shortly after we left the center, a garage owner, Jim Mould, hired me as a mechanic. Jim and I remained friends for a long time. Sadly, he passed away a few years ago.

Karen became pregnant and in September 1971 our son Shayne was born. That birth was a good time for us. We did it well. I was in the delivery room and worked with Karen's determination to do it naturally, using the Lamaze breathing technique. She says that I was the first father present at delivery at Regina General Hospital. Whatever the case, our son is the legacy of all that was loving and good about our relationship.

After Shayne was born, we bought a small house, a better car and tried to make the marriage work. Karen finished her studies at the university, got a degree and found a job. We bought a bigger house. But, as the years passed, our relationship did not improve. It got worse. About the only good times were our vacation trips, when we somehow came back together as a happy couple.

Part of the reason our relationship continued to deteriorate was that I didn't know how to articulate my feelings, even when I wanted to, and there were times when I did want to. My upbringing may have had something to do with my inability to express myself. There was little of that kind of expression at home. My mother was rather stoic. She tried to keep a lid on my Dad and his emotions, so about the only time I ever saw feelings expressed was when my

Dad blew the lid off in a verbal explosion of anger. Karen, on the other hand, knew how to express herself well and that made me feel even more defensive.

By the summer of 1976, our marriage was a shambles and there was no hope of restoring it. We could no longer find any common ground. There had been too much pain and abuse. We separated and were divorced soon after.

That was a hard time for me. Messed up as our marriage had been, it was still a safer place to be than in my earlier struggles with the U.S. Army. Without it, I was scared stiff.

AMNESTY 1977

For the next year or more I pretty much drifted. I spent too much time at the bar and far too much time chasing women. My job as a mechanic kept me going on a modest income, but I no longer had much inspiration for getting down and dirty in the grease.

In the spring of 1977, my Mom called to tell me they had received a letter from the Army saying that I might be eligible for discharge under a program instituted by President Jimmy Carter. Having already rejected President Gerald Ford's so-called amnesty—the one where alternative service was required—I was at first unimpressed by this latest offer.

But Mom gave me a phone number to call at Fort Benjamin Harrison, Indiana and asked me to call and find out about the program. I had heard about a new offer to draft dodgers, but nothing about an amnesty for deserters, so I asked Mom to check it out with the amnesty people she had been working with, to make sure it was legitimate. I wasn't trusting the U.S. government, but it turned out to be for real. Although still wary I called the number in Indiana. They asked me a few questions they used to identify callers then told me I would receive more information by mail. A short time later I received a letter saying I was eligible and I should report to Fort Benjamin Harrison on a specified date. The letter would be my passport into the United States, presumably because I was on a wanted list.

The amazing turn in all this is the role my Mom was playing. Both my parents had undergone a major transformation.

My Mom first went to bat for me in 1970, when I asked her to get a grade transcript from Springfield High School. I was thinking of attending the Saskatchewan Technical Institute in Moose Jaw. The high school refused to give her my transcript. School Superintendent Sydney Pierce would not give her a reason for refusing to release the transcript. All he said was, "This case is different."

So Mom got in touch with the National Council of Churches, which notified the Vermont branch of the American Civil Liberties Union. ACLU attorney William Moeser took the case. He threatened the school board with legal action if it did not review my request and act accordingly. The ACLU said there was a precedent in Michigan. The attorney general there had ruled that transcripts were the personal property of the student and it was illegal and unconstitutional to withhold them.

One of the school board members was the father of one of my best friends in high school, Russ Shaw. Richard Shaw declined to comment on the case, and it was later reported that he had told his children never to have contact with me again. Russ has assured me since that that was unsubstantiated rumor, and that to the contrary both his parents were relatively understanding of what I was doing.

Pierce refused to give Moeser the transcript, but a week or so later faced with possible legal action, the board found some wiggle room. It said that because I'd turned twenty-one, the school could release the transcript only upon a personal request from me. Moeser said that was "a lot of foolishness" designed to penalize me because I had deserted. But eventually the school sent the transcript directly to me in Regina, defusing what the *Rutland Daily Herald* said "could have been a boiling local controversy."

For my parents, that was probably the first turning point. The second one came in December 1973, when Gloria Emerson interviewed them for the *New York Times*. My father had retired and they moved to Sharon, Vermont, because it was closer to the White River Junction veterans hospital where Mom was still working. Emerson had spent time in Vietnam and she knew what she was talking about. She wrote that as Christmas approached, few people in Sharon had much to say about Vietnam: "But, as in every corner of the United States, there are middle-aged parents whose family gatherings at Christmas are never complete. These are the ones whose children are not coming home, and whose lives have been forever changed by a war in a country they cannot imagine.

"In a mobile house, off Route 14, the Vietnam war has not ended at all for Mr. and Mrs. Rennie (sic) Perrin, a couple with quiet and orderly ways."

Emerson went on to tell my story and the story of how my parents had struggled to cope with what I had done: " 'It's awfully hard for people to understand,' Mr. Perrin said. 'When this first happened we didn't go along with Dick because we didn't understand it. Like most people don't.'

"It wasn't until three years ago that both came to the conclusion their son was right to desert.

"Neither likes to speak of the cruelties, intentional or coincidental, shown to them by friends or acquaintances. They are not complainers. They speak, instead, of the good reactions from other Vermonters."

Valley News, the daily newspaper across the river in Lebanon, New Hampshire, reprinted the article in its December 11 edition. Local reactions were mixed. One reader said that while he sympathized with my parents, there should be no amnesty for the likes of me. A woman wrote, "Richard deserted us and our men when they needed his assistance and support—and in my estimation he deserves NO aid from us—and, might I add, no publicity or sympathy."

A reader from White River Junction responded to her in a subsequent letter to the editor. He described the Vietnam War as an "obvious attempt to rule a small Asian nation by foreigners from halfway around the world. Some people sensed the injustice before it became popular to do so and we must reassure these people that they were correct. Richard Perrin was one of those people; he has suffered much for his decision; let us help him return and in doing so awaken the courage of our convictions."

Meanwhile, Emerson's article had been generating letters to my parents from all over the country. Most of the letters were favorable and a great consolation to my Mom and Dad, and I am very thankful to those writers, because I put my folks through hell. On the other hand, letters to my parents back in 1967 when the

Stokely interview aired, were certainly not favorable. Something had changed in the United States.

One long, thoughtful letter was from a psychologist and college professor living in Enfield, New Hampshire. He said Emerson's story was the best Christmas gift he could receive that year. "In matters of conscience," he wrote, "each person must decide for himself, and it was not my place to intrude in the commitment of another. But in my heart I said a little thank you every time a young man such as Richard had the courage to follow Thoreau's different drummer, to see beyond the slogans and calls to a narrowly define patriotism, and all too often, the official lies and deceptions, and to follow instead his own deeper commitment to life and to the sanctity of his fellow human beings."

Then there was a note from a Vietnam veteran living in Honolulu. He urged my parents to stand by me, saying he had "made the decision to go to Vietnam, but I harbor great depression and shame for my portion of that moment in my life."

More encouragement came from a minister in Vermont. He said he had been preaching to his congregation in favor of an unconditional amnesty: "Personally, I am proud of what your son did. His moral sensitivity and his willingness to risk exile and imprisonment to preserve it put the majority of Americans, especially us preacher-types, to shame."

And the mail kept rolling in. A Pennsylvania man said he had read the *New York Times* article: "My simple reaction to the abuse you and your children have had to endure is to state that your son, Richard, is one of the true heroes of the sordid mess known as Vietnam."

Writing from Kansas City, Missouri, a woman said an article in the *Kansas City Star* had caught her attention: "As our country whittles away at our civil liberties and the individual rights of humans, I hope you will retain your pride and love for the man whom you raised to stand fast to his convictions and beliefs. You must be truly wonderful people to have instilled these qualities in your son."

A woman from Hartford, Connecticut said she "could forgive Richard Nixon his many sins and crimes if he would declare amnesty for all. I'd even be willing to let him sit out the next three years in the shambles around him. But his greatest sin is that he has no compassion."

There was a letter from a young mother in Ossining, New York, a Christmas card from New York City, both wishing my parents well and hoping that our family would be reunited. A New Jersey woman said that her son—also named Richard—had been killed in Vietnam and his death had left a hole in her life that nothing would ever fill. She prayed that God would give "us all the strength to carry on, for what this Vietnam War did to our boys, and a useless war at that."

There was a poignant letter from an ex-Army captain who was staying at the Parkhotel Schönbrunn in Vienna, Austria. the *International Herald Tribune* had picked up Emerson's story. He said he had volunteered to serve in Vietnam "for the very same strong feeling that motivated your son to avoid Vietnam.... In that respect, we are both the same—each of us did what we felt was right. Your son's decision was harder than mine and I respect him for having listened to his conscience." He spoke of the loneliness of being away from home—a loneliness he was obviously feeling as he wrote—and said, "I can only ask that you not give up hope because eventually the people of this country will come to their senses and agree on an unconditional amnesty. I and thousands of other Vietnam veterans want to see our brothers come home as soon as possible."

Other letter writers were not as understanding. A soldier wrote from North Carolina urging my parents to advise me never to seek amnesty. "Vietnam may have been wrong, but Americans must never desert their Army in times of strife. Deserters and dissenters cost the lives of their fellow men in arms. Please accept the fact that your son is no longer worthy of American citizenship, not by chance but by choice."

About that time—acting in part out of a nagging fear that the U.S. government would one day convince the Canadians to kick me out—I decided to become a Canadian citizen. It is ironic that as I pulled back from politics my parents were becoming more deeply involved. They had begun quietly working for the unconditional amnesty that they had hoped would one day allow me to come home, at least for an occasional visit. They supported me completely when I decided not to accept President Ford's conditional amnesty in 1974. Ford's plan required war resisters to spend six to twenty-four months in alternative service.

A story in the September 23, 1974 *Daily Eagle* of Claremont, New Hampshire sums it up pretty well: "Perrin believed when he deserted from the United States Army in West Germany in 1967 that he was doing something morally correct," the *Eagle* story said. "To accept Ford's offer, which [Perrin] deems an offer of clemency, would be to admit wrongdoing where he feels there has been none. Ford does not offer amnesty, 'Amnesty by definition, means forgetting. Clemency means they are offering us an opportunity to make up for what we did wrong,' Perrin said."

The story indicates that my parents were already pushing for an unconditional amnesty, even though they realized that I would probably never return to the United States to live. My Mom said Ford's offer was "good for the boys in prison in this country, but there is not much provision for the boys in Sweden, Canada, or other countries."

That same edition of the *Eagle* ran a letter to the editor from a local American Legion official: "We are against total amnesty in any form....

"We don't even go along with President Ford's conditional amnesty plan....

"First of all these war resisters have said right along, that they should be welcomed back to this country without having to serve in any capacity to the government, and they shouldn't even have to say they are sorry.

" Even a lot of parents of these resisters feel the same way, and have been putting on marches to this effect....

"I hope that you will notice in this letter that we haven't referred even once to these deserters as men.

"A man would never desert his comrades in action to let them die or lose their limbs or become disabled for the rest of their lives." Small wonder my Dad had stopped going to Legion meetings.

In February 1975, my parents attended a convocation of families of war resisters at Saint Mark's Episcopal Church in Washington, D.C. sponsored by the New York-based National Council for Universal and Unconditional Amnesty. The convocation brought together families from all over the country.

Former Attorney General Ramsey Clark spoke, along with a retired Marine Corps colonel who had been a prisoner of war in Hanoi for more than five years, and a former Green Beret named Gerry Condon, who had been AWOL for six years and had defiantly crossed the border from Canada, using a false ID.

Washington Post reporter Margot Hornblower interviewed my parents for a story she filed for the February 3, 1975 edition. Hornblower described my Dad as "a gentle looking man with wire-rimmed glasses." My Dad told her that he and Mom had been making the trek north every year to see me and they would do it as long as they could. "But I'm getting older," he said (he was sixty-five). "The day may come when we won't be able to go up and see him. We've told him, when one of us dies, not to come home. It wouldn't be worth the risk of getting picked up."

Hornblower pointed out that the families were there on behalf of the "12,500 deserters, 4,400 draft evaders [I think she meant 44,000] and the 8,700 young men already convicted of draft evasion who refused to serve in Vietnam and who—for the most part—are not responding to President Ford's amnesty program."

Also at the convocation was a schoolteacher from Massachusetts named Patricia Simon. Her son had been killed in Vietnam and she had formed an organization called Gold Star Parents for Amnesty. She said she wanted to counter the government's claim that amnesty could not be granted because so many of our sons had died in Vietnam. "Withholding amnesty does not bring back our sons," she said. "But it would end the suffering of our living sons. What better memorial could there be to our young dead soldiers than to forgive?"

"What disturbs me," my Dad told the *Post*, "is that people will not admit that the country was wrong. I can see through it because it happened to us." He had come a long way since 1967, when he was on national television condemning what I had done.

While they were in Washington, my parents lobbied the Vermont congressional delegation. They received a letter dated February 7 from Neal Houston, administrative assistant to Vermont Senator Robert Stafford:

> Following my very pleasant discussions with you last week, I did contact the Justice Department with respect to any individual who had deserted but is now a citizen of another

country and would like to return to the United States simply for a visit.

Unfortunately, I was advised rather strongly that if authorities were aware of his reentry into the country, he would be picked up and prosecuted.

I certainly am hopeful that this type of situation can be changed either through legislative action or executive order in the not too distant future.

I don't know where my folks came up with that angle. Not that I disapprove of the effort but I certainly would not have returned without an amnesty for everybody.

But my parents persisted. In the May 10, 1975 edition of the *Rutland Daily Herald*, they published a letter to the editor that again shows how far they had come:

The day after the unconditional surrender of South Vietnam, ending the war in that country, our son, Dick, called us from his home in Canada to give us some of his reflections on the end of U.S. involvement in the Vietnam conflict. He deserted the U.S. Army in September 1967, because he felt even then that our presence in Vietnam was wrong.

His first feeling, he told us, was one of jubilation that after 30 years, at least there was no more fighting in that country. Then, after a few moments of thought, he cried for the 56,000 men who lost their lives in Vietnam.

Dick has no feeling of malevolence toward those who served in Vietnam. He knows that in going to Vietnam they were doing what they thought was right. By the same token he feels in refusing to fight in this conflict that he was doing what he thought was right. He feels no remorse for his decision; in fact, in light of recent events in Vietnam, he feels a sense of having been absolved.

He has been out of this country for seven and a half years and has passed stiff requirements in order to become a Canadian citizen. He has a lovely Canadian wife and we have a nice little Canadian grandson. He has his own home and many friends....

We visit him annually and will continue to do so until we are physically or financially unable to do so. We hope before that time our country will have made an attempt to right her wrongs by allowing these men to make a choice, to return to America to live if they wish, without censure, and for those who desire to live and become citizens elsewhere, as our son does, visitation rights to America... These men who had the foresight to see only darkness at the end of the tunnel.

By December of 1975 the venerable *New York Times* columnist James Reston was calling for an unconditional amnesty at Christmas: "Before we come to an end of the old year, and go on to celebrate the 200th anniversary of the Declaration of Independence in 1976, is it not possible at least to think about an unconditional Christmas amnesty for the defiant exiles of the Vietnam War?"

After observing that Washington was "concerned at the moment for human liberty in Uganda, but almost seems to have no concern or pity for its own forgotten children," Reston goes on to recall that, after the Civil War, President Andrew Johnson tried offering conditional amnesty, as Ford had done, but it was roundly rejected. Then, on Christmas Day 1868, more than three years after the war had ended, Johnson proclaimed an unconditional amnesty for all, "without reservation," and restored "all rights, privileges, and immunities under the Constitution and the laws which have been made pursuant thereof."

Reston points out that the root meaning of amnesty is not "forgiveness" but rather "forgetfulness." He admits that the "plight of the 100,000 or so Vietnam exiles is really no big political issue. It is a sad story but the nation is paying no attention to it. But coming into the bicentennial year, it could be put behind us with a Christmas amnesty. There are so many other more important questions, but none more human or tragic."

Reston concludes by reminding his readers that Ford began his August 1974 inaugural speech by declaring that "Our long national nightmare is over," and ten days later he told a Veterans of Foreign Wars meeting in Chicago, "The urgent problem is how to bind up the nation's wounds." "But," Reston concluded, "the nightmare won't really be over or the wounds really be bound up until our children can come home."

At about that same time, Republican Senator Edward Brooke of Massachusetts and Michigan Democratic Senator Philip Hart were sponsoring a measure that would legislate an unconditional amnesty. Brooke vowed to stump hard for the measure over the Christmas recess, when he knew more people would be willing to listen. A World War II veteran and the only black in the Senate at the time, Brooke said it disturbed him "to deny anyone the right to come home. We are more prone to forgive our enemies, the Germans, the Japanese, than to forgive our own sons, who wouldn't fight those who were defined as our enemies for a specific moral reason."

So the pressure mounted, but President Ford refused to budge. No doubt there were political considerations, because the 1976 presidential campaign was soon in full swing. The leading Democratic candidates, Hubert Humphrey and Henry Jackson, opposed an unconditional amnesty. Jimmy Carter the virtually unknown peanut farmer from Georgia favored a pardon, which implies wrongdoing and falls short of an amnesty.

On July 15, Ron Kovic, a disabled Vietnam veteran, presented the case for amnesty to the Democratic National Convention. He was introduced by Louise Ransom of Vermont, who lost a son in Vietnam. She was a friend of my mother and is now a friend of mine. Kovic was joined by alternate convention delegate and war resister Fritz Efaw. Actor Tom Cruise played Kovic in the movie "Born on the Fourth of July."

To the surprise of many, Carter won the nomination and the election and, as President-elect, announced that one of his first acts as president would be to unconditionally pardon the draft law violators. The other war resisters were not included and my parents, along with everyone else in the amnesty movement, knew they still had a lot of work to do.

In the December 12, 1976 edition of Vermont's largest newspaper, the *Burlington Free Press*, my parents published the letter that follows. They were responding to six person-on-the-street interviews the newspaper had published earlier. The question asked was, "What do you think about Jimmy Carter's statement that one of his first priorities when he assumes the presidency will be to pardon all draft resisters?" Five of those interviewed supported the idea, however tepidly. The sixth, a man from South Burlington, said he thought Carter's idea was "very wrong because I believe if we have another war, we'll never get anyone in the service. I don't think they should go unpardoned for life, but they shouldn't be pardoned this soon." Here is my parent's response:

> We were interested in the views of a few area people on the subject of amnesty. We are parents of a deserter who has been out of this country, in exile, for nine years.

149

One of your interviewees stated that he felt they should be able to come back, but not this soon. What is soon? We think nine years is long enough.

Dick was one of the early protesters. We did not understand his position in 1967. We are proud now that he was able to see (sooner than most) what a mistake this country was making.

As for getting anyone in the service in the event of another war; that is an irresponsible statement. If this country were fired upon (as at Pearl Harbor, 1941) or needed to be defended for any other obvious reason, we feel we would have the same surge of patriotism that existed at the time.

It has been determined by many, including government officials, that we had no business in Vietnam. How would this country have reacted if another country had marched in and taken sides during our Civil War?

We think there should be an unconditional amnesty for all who were involved in opposing the Vietnam War. This includes: Vietnam era veterans with less-than-honorable discharges, to be upgraded to honorable; draft nonregistrants; indicted or indictable draft resisters; convicted draft resisters; deserters-at-large; civilian resisters with criminal records, or still imprisoned; former Americans newly naturalized to other citizenships now excluded or excludable from the United States.

That was a remarkable letter, considering our ordeal together over the past decade. And it must have caught the newspaper's attention because on January 2, 1977 it published a long piece by staff writer Walt Platteborze headlined "Parents of War Expatriate Quietly Work for Amnesty." For me, it marked another milestone in the politicization of my parents.

"The Perrins don't have the style, appearance or backgrounds usually expected of political activists", Platteborze wrote. "They are solid family people who have worked for a living all their lives and take particular care to maintain a well-scrubbed home. Mrs. Perrin, 53, works at the Veterans Administration Hospital in White River Junction. Perrin seems to be a watchful man and a good listener, traits he may have developed while barbering throughout Vermont. They have four children.

"They were unquestioning believers in American military policy until after their son's desertion.

"When Dick first turned against the war he pleaded with us to understand how wrong the Vietnam War was. We didn't go along with it then, but then it turned out that everything he was saying was true,' Rene said. '... It took a long time for us just like it did for everyone else.'

" 'I was sure he was right well before Watergate, and that made us even more sure,' added Betty. 'Even senators and other officials were by then saying we shouldn't be in Vietnam, and by the time Nixon was pardoned we were very sure."

My Mom told Platteborze that they had "recently attended amnesty rallies in Washington, D.C., and Cambridge, Mass., and planned to attend a January 12 rally on the Dartmouth College campus in Hanover, New Hampshire, being organized by Vermont and New Hampshire amnesty activists.

"Even though she doubts her ability as a public speaker, Betty has agreed to say a few words on behalf of the cause, along with peace movement luminaries such as former Yale chaplain William Sloane Coffin," Platteborze wrote.

Organized as part of National Amnesty Week, January 9-15, the Dartmouth rally featured Coffin as the main speaker. According to a press report, he was joined on the speaker's bill by Vermont writer Grace Paley; Vietnam veteran John Moody; Norwich, Vermont minister James Todhunter and my Mom, "mother of a deserter living in Canada." Most of what Mom said in her short speech rehashed the points she and Dad had made in earlier press interviews. But she got up there and she spoke and that must have been another milestone in her life. She ended with this plea, which echoed a letter to the editor my parents had written in 1975: "Dick has been out of this country for over nine years and has passed stiff requirements in order to become a Canadian citizen. We visit him annually and, if necessary, will continue to do so until we are physically or financially unable to do so. It will not be necessary to visit him in Canada if this country will make an attempt to right her wrongs by allowing these men to make a choice: to return to America to live or visitation rights to America for those who desire to live and be citizens elsewhere, as our son does. A total unconditional amnesty next week will do this."

In his speech at the Dartmouth rally, William Sloane Coffin rehearsed the history of amnesty in American wars, beginning with

151

the so-called Whiskey Rebellion, when George Washington was still president. James Madison offered unconditional amnesty to deserters of the War of 1812, Abraham Lincoln to every soldier in the Confederacy, even those who had deserted the Union Army to fight for the South.

Sloane Coffin recalled speaking with members of Vietnam Veterans Against the War, who were embittered because the real war criminals, the U.S. policy makers, would never be prosecuted. He suggested to them that "it might be trial enough for our leaders to be left at the bar of history. That's where I thought everyone should be left, those who prosecuted the war and those that deserted it. That's where God left Cain. That's where Lincoln left every man who wore gray even if once he had worn the uniform of the Federal Army.

" 'With malice toward none and charity for all.' Lincoln knew that it was politically expedient for the nation to be generous and for that reason stands closer perhaps than any other president to the spiritual center of American history.

"I wish, publicly supported by his cabinet, President Carter could lead us back toward the center. To broaden his pardon for draft evaders to a universal amnesty might not be a popular move, but I think it could be a wise one. The generous self in each of us needs badly to be addressed."

But even as Carter was about to be sworn in that January, syndicated columnist Mary McGrory, a longtime supporter of an unconditional amnesty, was not hopeful. Massachusetts Senator Edward Brooke had managed to round up only five cosponsors for his amnesty bill. Most legislators were unwilling to go out on a limb.

"The last few weeks were the best that amnesty has had," McGrory wrote. "There was the wan hope that Gerald Ford might be moved to try for a glorious exit with an uncharacteristic action. His martial state of the union address extinguished that small candle. Brooke wrote to White House counsel Phillip Buchen seeking an audience for himself and Mrs. Hart [wife of Senator Philip Hart, an amnesty supporter who had recently died]. He has received no reply. The signs from Plains [Carter's hometown in Georgia] are equally negative.

"According to Atty. Gen.-designate Griffin Bell, there is some thought to granting relief for exiles who took Canadian citizenship and were, during the Ford years, classified as 'undesirable aliens' and so forbidden to visit their families [possible fruit of my parents' labor, along with a lot of other people].

"If Carter does not declare amnesty immediately, it probably will never happen. His wife said he will be criticized whatever he does, and she is right. But the heartbreak of the amnesty seekers might be something he could live with more comfortably than the rage of his homeland."

On January 17, my parents sent a brief telegram to Carter, asking him for an amnesty broad enough to allow me to come home to visit. The response was a generalized form letter.

But Carter did keep his campaign promise. During his first week in office, he pardoned nearly all Vietnam-era draft evaders. Deserters were not included, but Carter did order the Pentagon to study the possibility of pardoning Vietnam War deserters (only about 0.01 percent had deserted under fire). The furor that followed was predictable. In Vermont, American Legion and Veterans of Foreign Wars halls flew their flags at half-mast. Some members sent their military decorations to Carter in protest. My Mom wrote a letter to the editor saying "the information gathered about the Carter pardon of draft evaders might have more meaning if it were obtained from some place other than the service club bars."

One reporter interviewed my Mom for reaction and she handled it like a political pro: "For Mrs. Betty Perrin of Sharon, Carter's pardon did not wipe away the effect of the Vietnam War....

"Her son Richard deserted in 1969 (sic), and has spent the last eight years in exile in Canada. The pardon does not include him.

" 'We are disappointed the pardon did not include Dick,' she said Saturday evening. 'But we are very happy for the boys coming home and out of jail.'

"Asked if she was bitter at the limited pardon, Mrs. Perrin replied: 'We just feel disappointed... We tried not to build up our hopes so we wouldn't have to come down too far.'

"She termed the pardon a 'marvelous step forward,' and said she hoped it will be 'a wedge' towards a blanket amnesty that will allow her son to return home.

"Mrs. Perrin who works at the Veterans Hospital in White River Junction, said she hoped that once the 'outrage' over the pardon settled down, there will be a more open approach toward amnesty, so eventually her son can move back to Vermont.

" 'Some people feel he was a coward not to stay,' she said. 'It took us a long time to understand how he felt and how to feel kindly toward him, but now we have a lot of respect for him and what he did.' "

In that same report, David Ross, a Vietnam Veterans Against the War leader in Vermont, echoed my Mom's disappointment: "Like other activists across the country, [Ross] criticized Carter Saturday for pardoning the 'white middle or upper-class people who found a legitimate way out within the system,' and ignoring the 'lower middle-class and working people who didn't have friends to get them out.'"

Herbert Brucker, retired editor of the *Hartford Courant* (Connecticut) put it plainly in a column he wrote that winter: "The fact remains that war resisters—criminals all under our laws—were right and the United States government was wrong.

"When the whole business is finished, and forgiveness has been extended to all who deserve it, then this country will have said at least by indirection that the war was a mistake. Perhaps, in the end, the President and Congress will summon the candor and the strength to declare that truth right out in the open.

"Then, at last, we can lay the Vietnam War to rest."

We are in another millennium now, a new century, and it still has not been laid to rest. Maybe all the old hawks will have to die first, so a fresh generation can take a long look back and repudiate the terrible and unjustified devastation we leveled upon Southeast Asia and upon our own country.

As for me, I will never ask for forgiveness and I don't want to be insulted by any such offer. That is for the likes of McNamara and Kissinger. For themselves and their deceased cohorts Johnson and Nixon. They were the "leaders" who sent young Americans to Vietnam and they are the ones who should be held accountable for the terrible things that happened there, not the GIs who were just trying to stay alive nor the war resisters who were trying to keep them alive.

But in May 1977, armed with my official Army letter, I crossed back into the United States for the first time in ten years. During those ten years, I had developed a mistrust of nearly everything American. For me, driving up to the border station was... Well, it was like a Brandenburg Gate of sorts.

A border guard sauntered out and glanced at the front license plate of my truck as he came around to the driver's door. He was relaxed and friendly. He asked where I was going and why. I told him Fort Benjamin Harrison, Indiana, to be discharged from the Army.

"Oh," he said. "Have you considered the Reserves?"

"No," I answered, I hadn't.

"Well give the Reserves some thought," he said, "It's a good deal and have a good trip."

He must have thought I'd been stationed in Canada or something.

So I drove on and was almost surprised that in the USA the grass was still green, the sky still blue. That night I stopped at a campground outside of Minneapolis. This guy walked up to me and said, "Oh, you're from Saskatchewan. Good hunting up there." I didn't know what to make of it all. Maybe I suspected everyone would see "Deserter" written in scarlet letters across my forehead.

As it happened, my brother David was in graduate school at Indiana State University in Terre Haute and I had arranged to stay with him the night before my discharge appointment at Fort Benjamin Harrison. David showed me around the campus. I was particularly impressed by the size of the building where the famed Larry Bird played. We stood by the last row of seats and looked down on a court that from that distance looked not much bigger than a boxing ring.

The next day David came along with me to my appointment with the Army. He sat outside in my truck all morning until mid-afternoon as I went through the discharge procedure.

There was nothing remarkable about the day except the interview with an Army shrink. He was using a questionnaire with multiple choice answers. For damn near every question he asked me concerning the reasons I left the Army, and about my home life before that, there was no appropriate answer for him to circle. I ribbed him a bit about it and wondered why a professional psychologist was using such a limiting tool.

Finally, they issued me an undesirable discharge, suitable for framing, and I was out of there. After I got back to Saskatchewan I sent an appeal of that discharge to Washington and it was upgraded to general, under honorable conditions. Then I received a letter stating that the upgrade was rescinded. I don't know what kind of discharge they finally settled on. There was an amnesty but it certainly wasn't unconditional.

After finishing at the Fort it was still early enough for David and me to catch the last Indianapolis 500 time trials at the Speedway. The big race was only a week away. Man, do they motor around that track. I believe that the only thing I've always wanted to do and haven't is race cars. Legally that is.

That evening David took me to his favorite bar in Terre Haute. It was free pizza night. No wonder it was his favorite bar. We ate our fill and swilled some beer while I talked about my plan to drive to Vermont the next day. Dave had finished his final exams and had a few days to spare so that night decided he'd come along with me. "Hell," he said, "let's go now!" So 'round about midnight we took off in my pickup.

By then I was tired, so Dave drove the first stretch while I slept in the camper I had rigged up in the back of the truck. I wasn't worried about David's driving. In fact I had given him his first driving lesson when he was a kid and I was seventeen. In those days he was always asking me to "floor it." So I took him out to an open meadow in my '59 Plymouth, got him behind the wheel where he could hardly reach the pedals and said, "Okay, you floor it!" He tore around that field spinning out of control but he didn't let up on the gas until he was damn good and scared.

As we got closer to Vermont I was telling myself not to be disappointed because the state couldn't be nearly as beautiful as I remembered it. But, heading north along the Connecticut River on the eastern side of the state, I was spellbound. With the farms and forested hills, the villages nestling near the river, the landscape seemed even more strikingly beautiful than the memory I had carried with me for a decade.

I had never been to Mom and Dad's place in Sharon, which is about halfway between the Massachusetts state line and the Canadian border. We pulled into their driveway in the afternoon. I honked the horn and they came out for a teary welcome home. Having Dave there was a surprise and a good bonus for them.

As I indicated earlier, for the previous six years I had concentrated on living a "normal" life in Canada, trying to grant myself an amnesty, meaning, I was trying to forget. I virtually ignored the work my parents were doing to help bring about an official amnesty in the United States. It had been no way to show appreciation to them. I guess I was wrapped up in my own wounds and anger. I had a chip on my shoulder and I'm still trying to get rid of it. I haven't forgotten!

Anyway, in the days that followed, Mom and Dad drove me around Vermont, visiting friends, colleagues and relatives, showing off their prize, the fruition of their amnesty work. And, you know, I think they were proud of me.

REUNION USA   1996

Through the 1970s I served what I called an apprenticeship in being Canadian. That included my honing up on knowledge of Canadiana and the language (English), as written and spoken by my friends and neighbors. I was so good at it that some of those people had no idea that I wasn't born and raised in Canada.

By some who knew me and of my past I was regarded as a good organizer. As a result, in the late '70s, I got a job managing a work/lifeskills training project for young law offenders sponsored by the John Howard Society. That was as a result of my experience working against the war in Vietnam. So even though I carried lots of emotional baggage from that time the outcome certainly hasn't been all bad.

In 1981, I was sitting in a small town restaurant and a group of eight or so were at the next table talking politics. I couldn't resist getting into it. We ended up pulling the tables together. One of the guys at the table, Reg Gross, was a cabinet minister in the provincial social democratic (NDP) government. At the end of the evening he invited me to a barbecue the next afternoon. At the barbecue we talked more and he offered me a job as an assistant (in U.S. parlance, an "aide"). That began a long association with the New Democratic Party. I worked as an assistant to members of the provincial legislature and to members of the federal parliament and as an organizer for the party between elections and as a campaign manager at election time.

Though he was certainly not a New Democrat, I even had the opportunity to work, for a day, with, or should I say for, Jean

158

Chrétien, now the Prime Minister of Canada. Back in 1969 he was in Pierre Trudeau's cabinet, so I thanked him for the immigration policy that allowed U.S. war resisters to stay.

For a few years, when he came to visit Saskatchewan, I worked as an assistant to Tommy Douglas, former Saskatchewan Premier and former leader of the federal New Democratic Party. I was working with Tommy when Mom and Dad came to visit in 1983. Tommy spoke at the national convention banquet. I took my folks to hear him. When he finished speaking, Dad said, "Jeez, he could have been president of the United States." I guess for Dad that was the ultimate compliment.

Tommy Douglas was small in stature but big in many other ways. He was a Baptist minister. Back in the 1930s, he got involved with what was called the social gospel. During the Depression, he was handing out food and clothes from the basement of his church in Weyburn, a town southeast of Regina, not far from the U.S. border. He got tired of watching that impoverishment and decided something had to be done about it, so he ran for Parliament as a member of the Cooperative Commonwealth Federation (forerunner of the NDP)—a coalition of left-wing farmers, workers and intellectuals.

He was elected to parliament and later on in the 1940s became provincial leader of the CCF. The party gained power in Saskatchewan in a sweeping victory over the Liberals in 1944. (Curiously enough, neighboring Alberta was suffering the same deprivation and a clergyman came to power there as well, but he was right-wing and the province has been right–wing ever since. I often refer to Alberta as "Texas North." There is lots of oil there and American influence has been much deeper than it has in Saskatchewan.)

Tommy was provincial Premier from 1944 until the early 1960s, when he resigned his provincial seat and became leader of the national party. In the 1960s, amid great controversy, Saskatchewan initiated what some called "socialized medicine." Liberals and Conservatives took up the increasingly popular cause and soon the whole country had it, although it varies slightly from province to province. The people pay for it indirectly through taxes, of course. So-called "sin taxes" are especially high. Cigarettes are about seven bucks a pack.

By the time I was driving Tommy around Saskatchewan he was getting on in years and he had long since resigned as leader of the NDP. He sat in the back seat of the car because his prostate cancer was painful and he needed space to stretch out. But the pain didn't keep him from telling me stories about his life in politics. Some of the stories were in the same vein as the one he told in many of his early political speeches. In that tale, he was helping out on a farm one day and ended up turning the crank on a cream separator. "My God," he said, "this is just like society. The farmers pour the whole milk into the separator, the workers turn the crank, the boss gets the cream and butter, the workers and farmers get the blue milk."

I asked him what he thought his greatest accomplishment was. Without hesitation, he said "rural electrification" back in the 1940s. His greatest failure? "I wasn't a good husband and father. I was preoccupied with politics." His daughter Shirley was married to actor Donald Sutherland and was involved with the Black Panthers in California.

During that NDP national convention in 1983, I escorted Tommy, his wife Irma and daughter Shirley to various functions. We left the convention one afternoon and Tommy said he wanted to see the hall where he would be speaking that evening. I took the three of them to the hall. Tommy and Shirley climbed up on the stage and Shirley said, "Daddy, this won't do." There was a big open space directly in front of the podium. People would be dancing there later in the evening, but nobody would be sitting there during Tommy's speech and he was the kind of extemporaneous speaker who needed eye contact with his audience. He asked me to see to it that some tables were moved into the vacant space. I took them to their hotel and raced back to the hall.

The national NDP organizer, Dennis Young, told me it would be impossible to move the tables because the logistics of serving food wouldn't work. So I waited until the national guys left to have a drink in a bar around the corner. Then I gathered a bunch of youngsters and moved the tables, lifted them up tablecloths and all and put them in front of the podium. When Dennis returned he was quite angry with me but he didn't have time to move the tables back.

I went to the hotel to get Tommy and the very first thing he said to me was, "Did you get those tables moved?" I said, "Yes, I did," and it was obvious he was pleased. My oldest child Shayne was along for that ride. I wanted him to meet a Canadian icon.

The speech Tommy gave that night was the one that blew Mom and Dad away. Dennis approached me the next day and apologized.

All of this was part of how I worked to become Canadian. But my roots were elsewhere and I doubt that I could have pulled them up even if I had wanted to. My mother died, and then my father, and still the roots were there, caught deep in the acid soil of Vermont. In the late 1970s, I joined my high school alumni association. When the invitation came for our thirtieth class reunion, I decided to go. I was apprehensive about it, but somehow it seemed to fit. It seemed to be part of the whole healing process.

So that June of 1996 I went to what was by then my brother David's camp on Lake Hortonia in west-central Vermont. This was the place where as a boy I had spent many happy hours with my Dad, finishing the cottage. My cousin Tim had agreed to help me with this book and he came over from New Hampshire for a few days so we could go over my first draft. That weekend we went to the reunion across the river in Charleston, New Hampshire.

A few days earlier, I had stopped in to see Art Davis, the man I worked for setting tile when I was in high school. He had lectured me then about "the virtues of the war in Vietnam," so it was with some trepidation that I went to see him. But Art's views had changed considerably. I told him I was nervous about the reunion. He told me not to be "because you have been absolved."

Tim and I were the first to arrive at the reunion. My apprehension had increased and I think Tim was nervous for me. We had a beer at the bar and the first guy from the class of '66 to turn up was a career Navy man, recently retired. That seemed to set the tone for the evening.

Fortunately, my high school friend Russ Shaw showed up a short time later. He was still slim, still crackling with the musical energy that had marked his life. We went out and sat at a table on the terrace so Tim could interview him. Much of that interview was lost because of a faulty tape, but Russ filled it in later with some written testimony. Most of what follows is adapted from that.

As I recall, I met Dick in 1960, in a seventh-grade math class taught by Mrs. Doten. We sat next to each other. His Dad was my barber. In those junior high years, we mostly rode bikes around looking for girls. We stood around at dances, went to dumb movies, played trombone in the band. That was about it.

Later, in high school, we talked while listening to the Beatles or We Five. We went hunting for everything and never shot anything. We drove around in Dick's latest, soon to be restored or customized vehicle, usually on the road, but once or twice on lawns and through at least one garden. We talked about cars, music, girls, seldom anything serious such as politics, until our senior year.

The first I knew that Dick was even aware of that sort of thing was when he came back from visiting his older brother in Chicago and had been in a civil rights march. I was in a liberal-thinking youth group at the time, so I had enough background information to know what he was saying, but I didn't have a passion for it like Dick did.

In our senior year, I was in a sociology class with Dick and that was the only time I heard him talk in school. I remember being amazed, even though we had talked about it before, at how much he knew about civil rights and the peace movement. I think the whole class and the teacher saw a whole new side of Dick that day.

Then school ended. I went to work nights in a factory to earn college money and Dick went to California. I didn't see Dick again until after he had enlisted in the Army, something I never thought he would do. It must have been when he was on his way to Germany. He stopped in at the factory to say goodbye. He was in uniform, shiny black shoes and all, and we stood on the railroad tracks outside the factory and talked for a few minutes. I remember feeling weird, uncomfortable. We hadn't spent much time together for a long while and we were heading off in different directions. But I didn't think it would be more than ten years before we saw each other again. It must have been then that he told me about being in the slammer at Fort Sill. I recall thinking that he was going to get himself in deep shit.

News came slowly about his going AWOL in Germany. It sunk in one night in school when I stopped in the TV room to watch the news with my political science major roommate. I think it was the only time I watched TV in all five years of college, and there on the news, behind a sheet, was Dick's voice explaining what they were doing in the antiwar movement in Paris.

I was confused. I wasn't doing well in school. All I wanted was to play my guitar or piano and write songs. I had already quit ROTC because I just didn't fit in with that group. I thought that if it came down to it I would try to get to Australia, probably because it was as far away as you could go and it seemed like a good place to get lost.

Because I was doing so poorly in school, they decided to draft me sometime in 1967. The letters and hearings went on for months. Eventually I had to go for a physical, which I failed with the help of an "independent consultant specialist" doctor, an older gentleman from Bangor, Maine (where I was going to school) who happened to not be favorably inclined toward war.

I was off the military hook, but no less confused. I had thought the government was good. I thought they knew what they were doing, that they had my interests in mind, that they were honest. That was what they said in school and my parents had always said so.

Now there was Dick, whom I knew, whom I respected, who had never lied to me—and he was

163

saying no, that is not the case, pay attention. Then I saw the draft board tactics for myself and even my parents seemed to be wondering what the hell was going on.

Home from school during one vacation, I stopped by the high school. My Mom worked in the office there. No students were around, but a few teachers were there. I dropped in on my history teacher. Such timing. He was in heavy conversation with an officer from military intelligence. My teacher looked up and said, "Oh, this guy was his best friend. You can talk to him." I was asked to wait in the office until they finished. I recall vividly my Mom saying quietly, "Don't tell them anything they can use against Dick." That's when I knew the country was really out of control.

After that the news about Dick was really sparse. I heard he was still in France, or maybe Sweden. Then somebody heard he was in Canada. I figured I'd never hear from him again.

What did I really think at the time? I'm not sure now. In retrospect, it's easier to see what was going on, but back then I was really torn. I did believe that Dick knew what he was doing, and that there had to be real facts behind what he was saying, because that's the kind of guy he was. He was not out for publicity on some sort of anti-authority trip. I believed all that.

When I became an art major, a real departure for me, I met more people who convinced me that Dick had the facts right, and more of us needed to join in to set it all straight. But I still wanted to believe everything I had been taught about the country that my ancestors had had such a large role in founding. I wanted to believe that the government wouldn't lie to its own people. I didn't think that riots and blowing things up were the way to get a point across. I wanted to believe that the system would work it all out, that someone would

*come along and get elected and just do the right
thing. I'm afraid that after a while I tried to ignore
the whole mess.*

*I got married, graduated, got a job teaching
in a private school (a world of its own), got
divorced, quit teaching, lived on my motorcycle for
a year—long hair, Fu Manchu mustache, played the
guitar, wished I had someone who understood
where I was at.*

*Then, around 1977 or 78, I was working as
a motorcycle mechanic and living in a shack in New
Hampshire. Dick stopped in. It was after the
amnesty and he was visiting, but he wasn't coming
back to stay. Our visit was short, but at least we
figured out how to stay in touch. Our first real sit-
down-and-get-caught-up talk wasn't until almost
twenty years later, in 1996, when we spent a couple
of evenings together and went to our thirtieth high
school reunion (where I was interviewed for this
book). I enjoyed the reunion, but Dick never did get
comfortable with the whole thing. I know some
people were glad to see him. Others, I guess, were
not. He probably won't go again.*

*Sometimes I think of Dick's Dad's quote in
the* Springfield Reporter *from some interview back
around 1967: "Who knows, maybe someday we'll
all think Dick was right." Well, a lot of us do. But
there is still a way to go.*

Russ is right. I never did get comfortable with that reunion.
It was the big "guess who he/she is game." I didn't recognize
many faces or names even. That Springfield world is almost from
another life, before I was reborn into another world. I like to drive
through Springfield when I visit Vermont but it's odd to feel like a
foreigner in your hometown.

One of the few people I recognized at the reunion was Nola
Yasinski. She overlapped a bit into my second life. She was the
only person from my high school days to write a letter of support
when I lived in Paris. I thanked her and tried to have a

165

conversation with her, but she was cool and seemed uncomfortable. Maybe she perceived my eagerness as a pass, which it certainly wasn't.

Though she wasn't there, I had hoped to see Barb Allen. Barb and I dated a couple of times back in 1966. One evening we went over to the Hampton Manor in New York and I've always regarded that as the best date I ever had. Jeez, I had a good time that night.

When we were asked to be seated for dinner, I sat in the nearest empty chair. There were three others at the table—Wayne Knox and his wife and another Vietnam veteran. Wayne's opening remark was: "Dick Perrin. Don't I remember seeing your picture in the *Rutland Herald*? Tass [Soviet news agency] wire photo wasn't it?" The conversation went downhill from there.

Our master of ceremonies for the evening was a former teacher at Springfield High, Harold Vincent. He is also the father of a classmate, Ralph Vincent. Ralph didn't attend the reunion.

At one point, Harold Vincent talked of the difficult times we moved into from high school. He asked how many of us had served in Vietnam and several hands went up. Then he asked how many had protested the war in Vietnam. I raised my hand. No one else did. That amazed me.

When we read about the Sixties, watch a movie or TV documentary about the Sixties, young people are protesting the war in Vietnam. Yet, out of perhaps one hundred of my classmates who graduated with me in 1966, only one hand was raised. Can that be possible?

Russ and I had a pleasant but brief conversation with Bonny Byington.

I exchanged a few brief words with Judy Grimes and I wanted to talk with her but I just had to get out of there. I left early.

Maybe I was trying to come full circle by attending that reunion, but somehow the circle did not quite close. It seemed that even there among my classmates I was still in exile. I don't think I will ever be wholly united with my homeland. Some might call that estrangement still another casualty of the war in Vietnam, and I'm sure that in that lingering sense of exile, at least, I am not alone.

Some healing has happened since that abominable war ended a generation ago. My hope is that this book will in some small way play a part in that ongoing process. Sometimes being right is not enough.

All letters and quoted news media material in this book, as well as other archival material related to Dick Perrin's story are located in the William Joiner Center Collections, Archives and Special Collections Department, Healey Library, University of Massachusetts Boston, Boston, MA 02125.   (617) 287-5850
http://www.lib.umb.edu/archives/perrin.html

hoka hey

Index

Printed in the United States
By Bookmasters